蟬丸源氏物語

「源氏物語」は読むほどに、とても奥深いということがわかります。
そこには、若い頃に読んだ通り一遍の知識とは違うものが、どっしりと横たわっていました。
恋愛だけでなく、政治や宮中の仕組みなども盛込んであります。
一番有名な最初の頃の、ハリウッド映画のような一大スペクタル巨編も楽しくて良いけれど
女三の宮の登場する第2部は重くて深くて、中年の源氏の心情がリアルに描かれています。
その後の宇治十帖は小説のようで、登場人物の内面を掘り下げています。
作者の紫式部の年齢と共に、内容が「物語」から「小説」へと進化していったようです。

「源氏物語」は大人のドラマで、深く重い部分もありますが、これを猫で表現すると、
ファンタジーの世界が出来、人間であれば生々しいものも、猫ならソフトになります。
そして、そのラインの美しさ。
平安時代のお約束の、十二単衣も長い黒髪もありません。

蟬丸流「蟬丸源氏物語」をご覧下さいませ。

When I reread The Tale of Genji and find its profoundness every time.
There lies a pile of factors I could not find when I read in my school days.
The tale is not like the image from its formal knowledge or preconception.
Not only love-romance, there are politics and tradition in the Imperial Court in the tale..
I like part I, the most famous and enjoyable part, because of it is similar to the spectacle movies of Hollywood, but I love part II that Princess Onna-san-no-miya appears. The plot is sarious and deep, and Murasaki pictured the mind of Genji in his middle age realistically..
The following part III, Uji Chapters, she wrote the minds of every characters vividly like modern literature.
Murasaki reached her maturity and Genji is also matured----from tale to novel.

The Tale of Genji is a drama for adults and it has depth and weight, but when I make the all charcters to cats, it became a fantastic world. You can see graphic descriptions of human deed change into cats' mellow behavior.
And cats have neither Juuni-hitoe, twelve-layered ceremonical kimono, nor long black hair, but their beautifully smooth shapes.

Please see and enjoy The Tale of Genji of Semimal---- Genji in Semimal style.

源氏物語

　十一世紀、平安中期に紫式部によって書かれた全五十四帖からなる長編物語で、桐壷帝の第二皇子として生まれた聡明で美しい光源氏の奔放な恋愛、地位、権力闘争などを交えた、その子孫の恋愛物語までの絢爛豪奢な王朝を舞台とした物語です。
　平安貴族社会を中心とした恋愛感や結婚・権力・信仰などの社会構造、生活様式などが全てに盛込まれ華麗な宮廷生活と当時の女性達の在り様などが描かれています。

The Tale of Genji

The Tale of Genji is a novel composed of as many as 54 chapters, authored by Japanese noblewoman Murasaki Shikibu in 11th century, or the middle of the Heian period.
This novel is set in the magnificent Imperial Court and depicts the life of Hikaru Genji a smart, good-looking prince of Emperor Kiritsubo,
focusing on his wild romances and struggles for position and power as well as the love stories of his descendants.
Covering all aspects of the Heian aristocracy including the views on love, social structures such as marriage, power, religion and lifestyles, this long novel also pictures the gorgeous lives in the Imperial Court and how women in those times led their lives.

参考文献：『新編日本古典文学全集 源氏物語』(小学館)、『源氏物語』円地文子訳(新潮文庫)

源氏香

　源氏香とは組香（何種類かの香りを組合わせて、その香木の香りを嗅ぎ当てる遊び）の一つです。

　源氏香では五種類の香木を五包ずつ合計二十五包を混ぜ合わせ、そこから無作為に選んだ五包を順に焚き、香席に五回、聞香炉が回されます（香りは「聞く」と言います）。

　客は右から順に縦線を書いた紙を持ち、香りを聞いたら同じ香りと思うものは、縦線の上の部分を横線で繋ぎます。五回香りを聞いたその後に出来た図を源氏物語の巻名にあてはめられた「源氏香の図」に照らし合わせて、巻名で答えて遊びます。

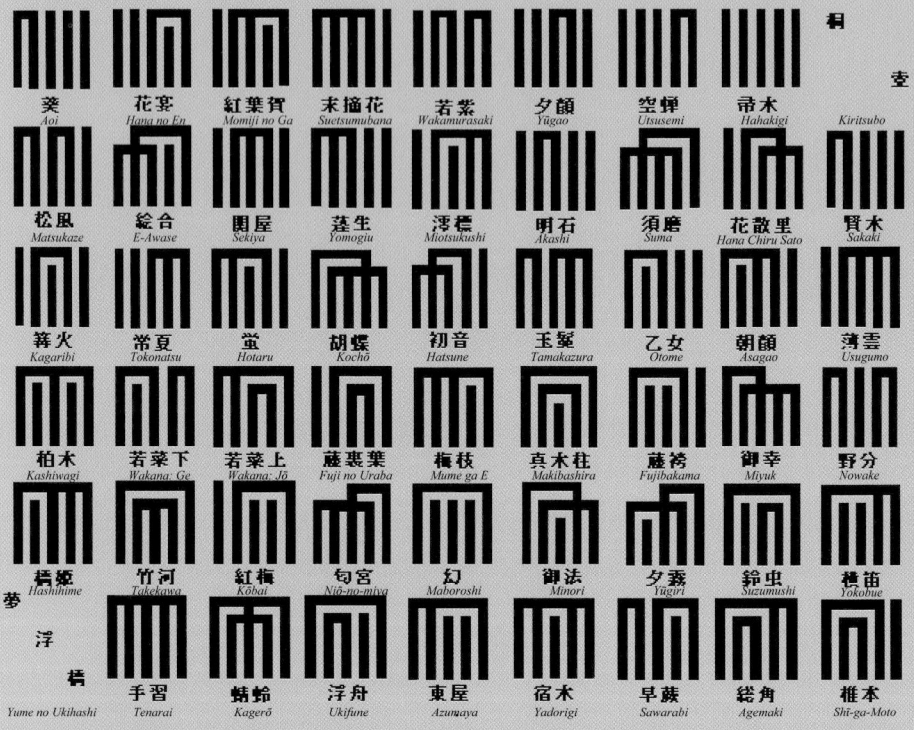

Genji-kō

Genji-kō is an old game of scenting out the smells of five pieces of fragrant wood.

The player scenting the fragrances draws the result in a pattern and gives the answer by representing the obtained pattern by the name of one of the chapters of the Tale of Genji as shown in the "Genji-kō Patterns" below.

Genji-kō is one of the games of Kumiō (combing some incenses and telling the incenses used by smelling the combined fragrance). With Genji-kō, five kinds of fragrant woods are mixed into twenty-five packs composed of five packs each of five incenses, five packs are selected at random and burnt in sequence. The incense burner is passed among the players for five times. (In Japanese, act of smelling a fragrance is expressed as listening to a fragrance.)

Each player is given a sheet of paper on which five vertical lines representing each turn of incense burners are drawn. After listening to each incense, the player connects the tops of the vertical lines that the player finds to have the same incense. After five times of listening, the player answers the name of the obtained pattern by representing it with the name of one of the chapters of the Tale of Genji by referring to the "Genji-kō Patterns".

第一部 Part I

第一帖　桐壺 (きりつぼ)

尋ねゆく　まぼろしもがな つてにても　魂のありかを　そこと知るべく

桐壺帝

（亡き更衣の魂を捜しに行く幻術師がいてほしいものよ、そうすればその魂のありかをどこぞと知ることができるだろうに）

　最愛の桐壺更衣を失った桐壺帝は、風の音や虫の音につけても、ただ無性に哀しいお気持ちでした。源氏の母・桐壺更衣は、高い身分でもないのに帝の深い愛を受けたため、多くの女性の嫉妬を集めて源氏が幼い時に亡くなり、桐壺帝の嘆きは続きます。
　桐壺更衣に似る藤壺の宮を妻に迎えるまで。
　そして源氏は亡き母の面影を求めて藤壺を慕うようになっていきます。

Chapter 1　Kiritsubo (Paulownia Court)

[Emperor Kiritsubo] Tazuneyuku / Maboroshi mogana / Tsute nite mo / Tamano arika o/ Soko to shirubeku
 (I wish there were a wizard to search for my late Kōi, then I would be able to know where her spirit is.)

After losing his beloved Kiritsubo Kōi, Emperor Kiritsubo has been lost in grief even when hearing the sound of wind or singing of instincts.
Kiritsubo Kōi, mother of Genji, was loved deeply by Emperor though she was not of noble birth. Because of it, she excited jealousy of many women and died when Genji was just an infant.
The grief of Emperor Kiritsubo continues until he marries Fujitsubo, a lady who resembled Kōi.
Meanwhile, Genji heightens feelings for Lady Fujitsubo because of her resemblance to his late mother.

第二帖　帚木 (ははきぎ)

帚木の　心を知らで　園原の　道にあやなく　惑ひぬるかな　　源氏

（そこにあるかと近づくと見えなくなる帚木のように、つかむことの出来ないあなたの心を追って、私は空しく迷っています）

　五月雨の降るある夏の夜、源氏のいる宮中の宿直所に訪れた頭の中将と話が弾み、いつしか話題は女性論へ。そこに左馬頭や籐式部丞も加わって、女性談議に華が咲きます。
　嫉妬深い女、浮気な女、内気な女、…「雨夜の品定め」が盛上がります。

Chapter 2　Hahakigi (Broom Tree)

[Genji] Hahakigi no / Kokoro o shirade / Sonohara no / Michi ni ayanaku / Madoinuru kana
(Pursuing your heart like the broom tree that vanishes on approach, I am bewildered vainly on the road to Sonohara.)

One rainy night in early summer, a friend (Tō no Chujō) of Genji visits the night-duty room in the Court to see him. Before long, the topic of their chat moves on to the subject of women. Two other friends (Hidari no Uma no Kami and Tō no Shikibu no Jō) join them, and their talk comes down to the judgment and grading of women.
There are jealousy women, fickle-minded women and shy women – this is the famous "Discussion on a Rainy Night".

第三帖 空蟬 (うつせみ)

方違えで宿泊した紀伊守の屋敷で、その父の若い後妻と一夜を過ごした源氏。もう一度会いたいと忍んで行ったところ、彼女は寝所から消えてしまいます。後には蟬の抜け殻のような着物と温もりが残っていただけでした。

空蟬の 身をかへてける 木のもとに なほ人からの なつかしきかな 源氏
(蟬が殻を脱ぐように、薄衣を残して消えたあなた。この衣の匂いはこんなになつかしいのに)

空蟬の 羽におく露の 木がくれて しのびしのびに ぬるる袖かな 空蟬
(空蟬の羽に置く露が人に見えぬように、忍んでは涙に濡れるわが袖よ)

Chapter 3 Utsusemi (Cicada Shell)

Following a fortune telling about bearing, Genji stays at the mansion of the Governor of Kii and spent a night with the young wife of the father of the Governor.
But, when he visits her in secrecy another day, he finds she has fled from her bedroom.
The only thing left there was her garment like a cicada's shell, with some warmth of her body.

[Genji] Utsusemi no / Mi o kaetekeru / Ko no moto ni /Nao hitogara no /Natsukashiki kana
 (Empty cicada, you have gone leaving your shell under the tree. Only the scent of this human husk makes me miss you so much.)

[Utsusemi] Utsusemi no /Ha ni oku tsuyu no /Kogakurete / Shinobi shinobi ni / Nururu sode kana
 (Like dewdrops on the wings of empty cicada are invisible under the tree, my sleeves grow damp with my tears when I hid in secrecy.)

15

第四帖　夕顔 (ゆふがほ)

　心あてに　それかとぞ見る　白露の　光そへたる　夕顔の花　　　夕顔
　　（あのお方でしょうか？白露の美しさでこちらの夕顔の花もいっそう美しくなります）

　寄りてこそ　それかとも見め　たそかれに　ほのぼの見つる　花の夕顔　　　源氏
　　（もっと近くに寄って、はっきりとお目にかかりたい。夕暮れ時にぼんやりと見た花の夕顔を）

　源氏は乳母の病気見舞いの折、隣家に咲く白い花に目を留めます。花の名前を尋ねると、白い扇に夕顔の花を載せてさし出されました。扇は粗末な家に不似合で、持ち主の移り香が深くしみこみ、歌も上品で奥ゆかしい感じです。興味をそそられた源氏は、内気で頼りなげなおっとりとしたこの女性に、不思議なほど惹かれます。
　ある朝、夕顔と別れたくない源氏は人気のない廃院に彼女を誘い、愛の時間を過ごします。しかしその夜、源氏は不気味な夢を見て飛び起きると、夕顔は源氏の腕の中で冷たくなっていくばかりでした。

Chapter 4 Yūgao (Evening Glory)

[Yūgao] Kokoroate ni / Sore ka to zo miru / Shiratsuyu no / Hikari soetaru /Yūgao no hana
(I guess you are that man. The flower of my evening glory flower gets more beautiful by the shine of white dew.)

[Genji] Yorite koso / Sore ka to mo mime / Tasogare ni /Honobono mitsuru /Hana no yūgao
(I want to get closer to see your face, the evening face of the flower I could see only vaguely in the dusk.)

Genji visited his nurse who fell ill and notices a white flower in the neighbour's garden.When he asks the name of the flower, the neighbour woman offers him flower of evening glory on a white fan.The fan is unfit to the humble house. It has deep scent of the fragrance of the owner, and her poem is also graceful and well-polished. Genji is strangely attracted by this shy, seemingly weak and rather slow-tempo woman called Yūgao.
On a morning, Gerji who is unwilling to leave her invites her in an abandoned temple and passed a moment of love. On the same night, Genji is suddenly woken up by a weird dream and finds that the body of Yūgao in his arm is getting colder and colder.

第五帖 若紫（わかむらさき）

手に摘みて いつしかも見む 紫の 根にかよひける 野辺の若草 源氏
（手に摘んで早く見たいものよ。紫草の根につながっているあの野辺の若草を）

源氏が十八歳の春、体調が優れず加持を受けるために赴いた北山で出会った少女は、源氏の慕う藤壺の宮の姪で、母を失い祖母の尼君に養育されているという。源氏はこの少女を身近に置いて、思いのままに育てたいと思いました。

Chapter 5　Wakamurasaki (Young Gromwell)

[Genji] Te ni tsumite / Itsushika mo Min / Murasaki no / Neni kayoikeru / Nobe no wakakusa
(I would like to pluck soon the field plant, whose roots are connected to the roots of gromwell.)

In the spring at the age of 18 years, Genji visited Kitayama to have an incantation for his ill health and met a girl who looks perfectly like Lady Fujitsubo for whom he harbors a secret love. The girl is actually a niece of Lady Fujitsubo. Genji hears that she lost her mother and is presently supported by a nun who is her grandmother. Genji feels like growing her up to an ideal woman under his custody.

第六帖 末摘花 (すゑつむはな)

なつかしき 色ともなしに 何にこの 末摘花を 袖にふれけむ　源氏

(親しく心ひかれる色でもないのに、どうしてこんな末摘花に袖を触れてしまったのだろう)

源氏は荒れた邸に寂しく暮らしている故・日立の宮の姫君の話を聞き、興味を持ちます。彼女は古い邸で古い時間に住む古風な姫君でした。そしてその鼻は末摘花（紅花）のように赤かったのです。

Chapter 6 **Suetsumuhana** (Safflower)

[Genji] Natsukashiki / Iro to mo nashi ni / Nani ni kono / Suetsumuhana o /Sode ni furekemu
(This color is not the one I yearn for, but why do I bring my sleeve in contact with such a safflower?)

Hearing about the daughter of late Hitachi no Miya who lives alone in a dilapidated mansion, he is interested in her. She is an old-fashioned princess living in an old mansion and like in old time. Her nose was as rouge as the flower of suetsumuhana (safflower).

第七帖　紅葉賀(もみぢのが)

物思ふに　立ち舞ふべくも　あらぬ身の　袖うちふりし　心知りきや　　　源氏

（思い乱れて、とても舞う事など出来そうもない私が、あなたのために袖を打ち振ってお目にかけた、この心中をお察しくださいましたでしょうか）

美しい紅葉の季節に朱雀院への行幸がありました。
桐壺帝は身重でそれに出掛けられない藤壺のため、宮中で試楽を催し、源氏は青海波を舞います。
恋しい藤壺のために想いを込めた源氏の舞は格別に素晴らしく、人々の賞賛を浴びました。

Chapter 7　Momiji no Ga (Excursion for Autumn Leaves)

[Genji] Mono omou ni / Tachimaubeku mo /Aranu mi no / Sode uchifurishi / Kokoro shiriki ya
(I was so mixed up that I could not think how to stand up and dance, but I shook my sleeves for you. Did you understand how my mind was at that time?)

In the beautiful season of autumn leaves, Emperor has an excursion to the Suzakuin palace.
Emperor Kiritsubo holds a music and dance meeting in the Imperial Court for Lady Fujitsubo who cannot accompany him due to pregnancy. Genji performed the Seigaiha dance for her.
As Genji dances with deep feelings of his loving Fujitsubo, his excellent performance is praised by the audience.

第八帖 花宴(はなのえん)

あづさ弓 いるさの山に まどふかな ほのみし月の 影や見ゆると　　源氏
(ほのかに見た有明の月の姿がまた見られぬものかと、彷徨っております)

心いる 方ならませば 弓張の 月なき空に 迷はましやは　　朧月夜の君
(お心に掛けてくださるのなら、弓張月のない空でも、お迷いになることはないでしょう)

宮中での桜の宴の後、源氏は忍び入った弘徽殿で「朧月夜に似るものぞなき」と口ずさむ女性と出会い、一夜の逢瀬を持ちます。夜明けに名も聞けぬまま、扇を取り交わしてあわただしく別れた女性は弘徽殿の女御の妹で、この春東宮妃になる六の君でした。

Chapter 8 Hana no En (Cherry Blossom Festival)

[Genji] Adzusa yumi / Irusa-no-yama ni / Madohu kana / Honomishi tsuki no /Kage ya miyuru to
(I am wandering to see again the moon I had an opportunity of viewing faintly)

[Oborodukiyo-no-Kimi] Kokoro iru / Kata nara mase ba / Yumihari no / tsuki naki sora ni / Mayoha mashi ya ha
(If you care for me, you will not be lost even under the sky without the crescent moon)

After the cherry blossom viewing festival in the Court, Genji creeps into the Kokiden palace and meets with a woman who recites poem "There is nothing like a night with a hazy moon". He spent a night with her.
In the dawn, Genji left the palace hastily even without knowing her name but only exchanging fans with her. He later knew that she was Roku-no-kimi, who is a younger sister of the Lady Kokiden. She is going to be the spouse of the Crown Prince in this spring.

25

第九帖　葵 (あふひ)

影をのみ　御手洗川の　つれなきに　身のうきほどぞ　いとど知らるる　　六条御息所

（影を宿しただけで流れ去る御手洗川のような君のつれなさゆえに、わが身の不幸せが身にしみて分かってきます）

　前東宮の未亡人、美貌で才媛の六条御息所は、源氏がやっと口説き落とした年上の恋人でしたが、最近のつれない源氏に心を痛めていました。
　しかし賀茂神社の儀式にお供をする源氏の姿を一目見ようとひっそりと出かけたのに、後から来た源氏の正妻・葵の上の車に無理に押しやられたため、車も壊れて身分もばれて深く傷ついてしまいます。
　それ以来御息所は体調がすぐれず、心が浮遊するようになるのでした。

Chapter 9　Aoi (Hollyhocks)

[Rokujō Miyasu-dokoro] Kage o nomi / -gawa no /tsurenaki ni /mi no uki hodo zo /itodo shiraruru
(Because of your coldness like the Mitarashi River that flows away even a shadow cast on it, I well understand how miserable I am.)

Widow of the late Crown Prince, Lady Rokujō Miyasu-dokoro is known for her beauty and talent. She is older than Genji but became his lover as a result of his ardent advances. However, she has recently been distressed by the cold behaviours of Genji towards her.
She goes out in secrecy to see the figure of Genji who attends a ceremony held in the Kamo shrine, but she is hurt deeply there because her retainers lose the race for holding a place for the car by those of Lady Aoi, who was the legal wife of Genji. Her car was broken by being pushed forcedly by the car of Lady Aoi that arrived after her car, and her identity was made public by this incident.
Since then, she gets ill and her mind begins to drift.

第十帖 賢木 (さかき)

神垣は しるしの杉の なきものを いかにまがへて 折れる榊ぞ

六条御息所

(ここの神垣には訪れる目印の杉もないのに、どうおまちがえになって訪ねていらっしゃったのでしょう)

六条御息所は、源氏を忘れようと、娘が伊勢神宮の斎宮になるための伊勢下向に同行を決心しました。伊勢行の前に身を清めるための住居も野宮に移りますが、そこへ源氏が榊の枝を携えて訪れました。会うのを拒んだものの、源氏に未練のある彼女は最後の一夜を共にしてしまいます。そして御息所の苦悩は更に増すのでした。

Chapter 10 Sakaki (Sacred Tree)

[Rokujō Miyasu-dokoro] Kamigaki wa / Shirushi no sugi mo / Naki mono o / Ika ni magaete / Oreru sakaki zo

(The fence of the shrine does not have a signpost cedar tree, but what kind of mistake has made you visit this place?)

To forget Genji, Lady Rokujō Miyasu-dokoro decided to accompany the trip of her daughter who will visit the Ise shrine to become a vestal virgin princess. To prepare for the visit to Ise, she moves to Nonomiya for purifying herself, but Genji visited her with a branch of the sacred sakaki tree. She once refused him but, due to attachment to Genji, she eventually spend that night with him. This increased her anguish further.

第十一帖　花散里（はなちるさと）

橘の香を　なつかしみ　ほととぎす　花散る里を　たづねてぞ訪ふ　　　源氏

(昔の人を思い出させる橘の香りが懐かしいので、ほととぎすは橘の花の散るお邸をさがしてやってきました)

源氏は、煩わしいことが多くなったこの世を厭わしく思っています。
五月雨の晴れ間、源氏は故桐壺院の女御・麗景殿の邸を訪れました。麗景殿は妹で源氏の恋人の花散里と二人でひっそりと暮らし、橘が香りほととぎすの鳴く邸で源氏の訪れをさりげなく歓待し、ともに故院の昔を懐かしみました。

Chapter 11　Hana Chiru Sato (Village with Orange Blossoms)

[Genji] Tachibana no / Ka o natsukashimi / Hototogisu / Hana chiru sato o / Tazunete zo tou
(In nostalgia for the scent of orange bloom that reminds the person I knew in the past, the cuckoo has come to the village where orange blossoms fall.)

Genji is tired of this world due to increasing troubles.
On a shiny day in the rainy season, Genji visited the house of Lady Reikeiden, a widow of late Emperor Kiritsubo.
The lady leads a secretive life with her younger sister Hanachirusato who is a lover of Genji. Genji and Reikeiden welcomed Genji unceremoniously and cherish the memories of late Emperor in the house surrounded by the scent of orange blossoms and songs of cuckoos.

第十二帖 須磨(すま)

ふる里を いづれの春か 行きて見ん 湊ましきは 帰る雁がね

源氏

(故郷にいつの春になったら行けるかわからぬ身には、帰る雁が羨ましい)

桐壺院の亡き後、源氏は新帝の母・弘徽殿の女御の怒りに触れ、須磨の地に蟄居します。愛しい人達と別れの挨拶をして、わずかばかりの供人と京を離れます。須磨の佗び住まいの中では京の人達との手紙のやりとりが唯一の楽しみでした。

源氏から離れる人が多い中、古くからの友人・宰相の中将が須磨に忍んで訪れました。

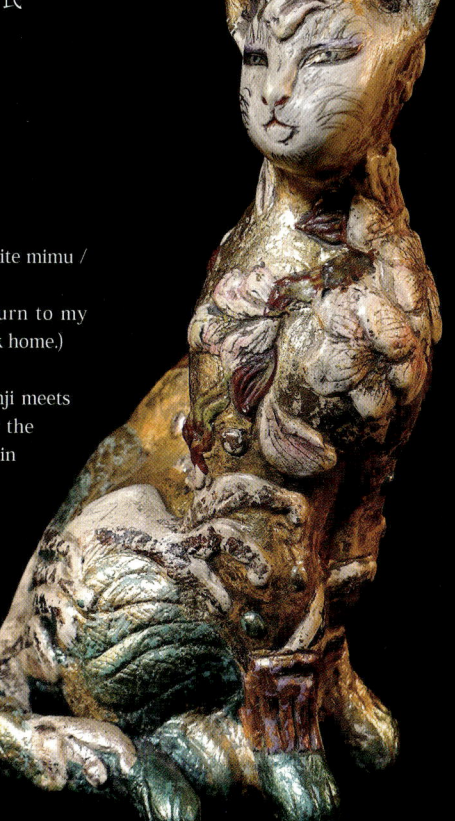

Chapter 12 Suma (Land of Suma)

[Genji] Furusato o / Izure no haru ka / Yukite mimu / Urayamashiki wa / Kaeru karigane
(Not knowing in which spring I can return to my hometown, I envy the wild geese flying back home.)

After the demise of Emperor Kiritsubo, Genji meets with anger of Lady Kokiden, who is now the mother of the new emperor, and is placed in confinement at the land of Suma.
He left the capital Kyoto with a few squires after making farewells to his loved ones.
The only distraction in the simple rustic life in Suma was exchanging letters with people in Kyoto.
While many people began to avoid contact with Genji, an old friend Tō no Chujō visited Suma secretly to see him.

33

第十三帖　明石 (あかし)

明けぬ夜に　やがて惑へる心には
いづれを夢と　わきて語らむ　明石の君

（明けることのない長夜の闇を迷っているこの私には、どれを夢と知り分けてお話することができましょう）

　激しい嵐が幾日も続き、源氏の夢枕に故・桐壺院が立ち、「この浦を去るように」と告げた翌朝、明石の入道が「夢のお告げで参りました」と船を仕立てて到着し、源氏は須磨から明石へと移り住みました。そこで都の女性にも劣らない入道の美しい一人娘・明石の君と出会い、二人は恋に落ちます。

Chapter 13　Akashi (Land of Akashi)

[Akashi no Kimi] Akenu yo ni / Yagate madoeru / Kokoro ni wa / Izure o yume to / Wakite kataran
(Wandering in the darkness of endless night, how can I speak by distinguishing which is dream and which is reality?)

After a heavy storm lasted for days, the late emperor Kiritsubo appears in a dream of Genji and tells him to leave the land of Suma. On the next morning, Akashi Nyudo visited Genji with a boat, saying "I've come here because I was told to do so by a dream". Genji decided to move from Suma to Akashi where Nyudo lives. In Akashi, Genji met the beautiful only daughter of Nyudo, named Akashi-no-kimi (Lady Akashi), who was not inferior in any way to Kyoto girls, Soon, Genji and her fell in love.

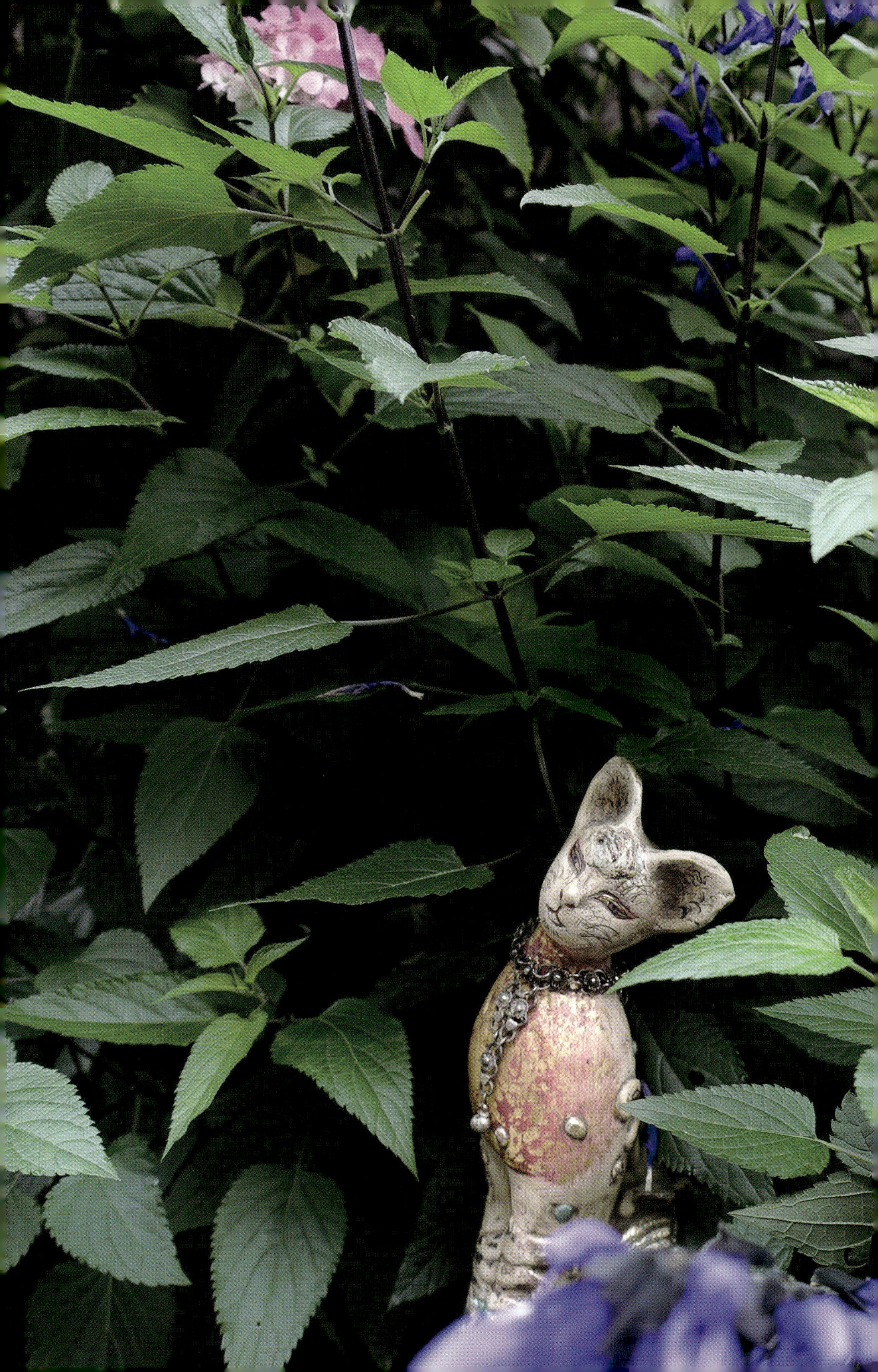

第十四帖　澪標(みをつくし)

みをつくし 恋ふるしるしに ここまでも
めぐり逢ひける 縁は深しな　　源氏

(身を尽くして恋い慕う甲斐があって、澪標にあるこの地でも巡り合った、あなたとの縁はとても深いのですね)

　源氏は京に呼び戻される事になりました。源氏は明石の君に想いを残しながらも帰郷し、明石の君は女の子を出産します。
　京では御代が変わり、源氏一門に再び春が巡ってきて、帰京後の源氏はとても忙しく、明石に行けません。明石の君は住吉詣の折に、源氏の一行に偶然行き合わせますが、その豪壮さに源氏との身分差を思い知らされ、参拝もせずに沈んだ気持ちで帰ってしまいます。

Chapter 14　Miotsukushi (Channel Buoys)

[Genji] Mi o tsukushi / Kouru shirushi ni / Koko made mo / Meguriaikeru / En wa fukashi na
(My utterly devoted love allowed me to meet you in this place with channel buoys. I realize how deep and fateful our karma is.)

Genji is eventually called back to Kyoto.
Genji returns home with a lingering affection to Lady Akashi, who gives birth to a girl after the separation. As the emperor has changed and the clan of Genji has become prosperous again, he becomes too busy to visit Akashi.
One day, Lady Akashi visits the Sumiyoshi shrine and encounters a party of Genji by chance. But the gorgeousness of the party let her realise the status distinction between them. Discouraged, she returned home without offering prayers at the shrine.

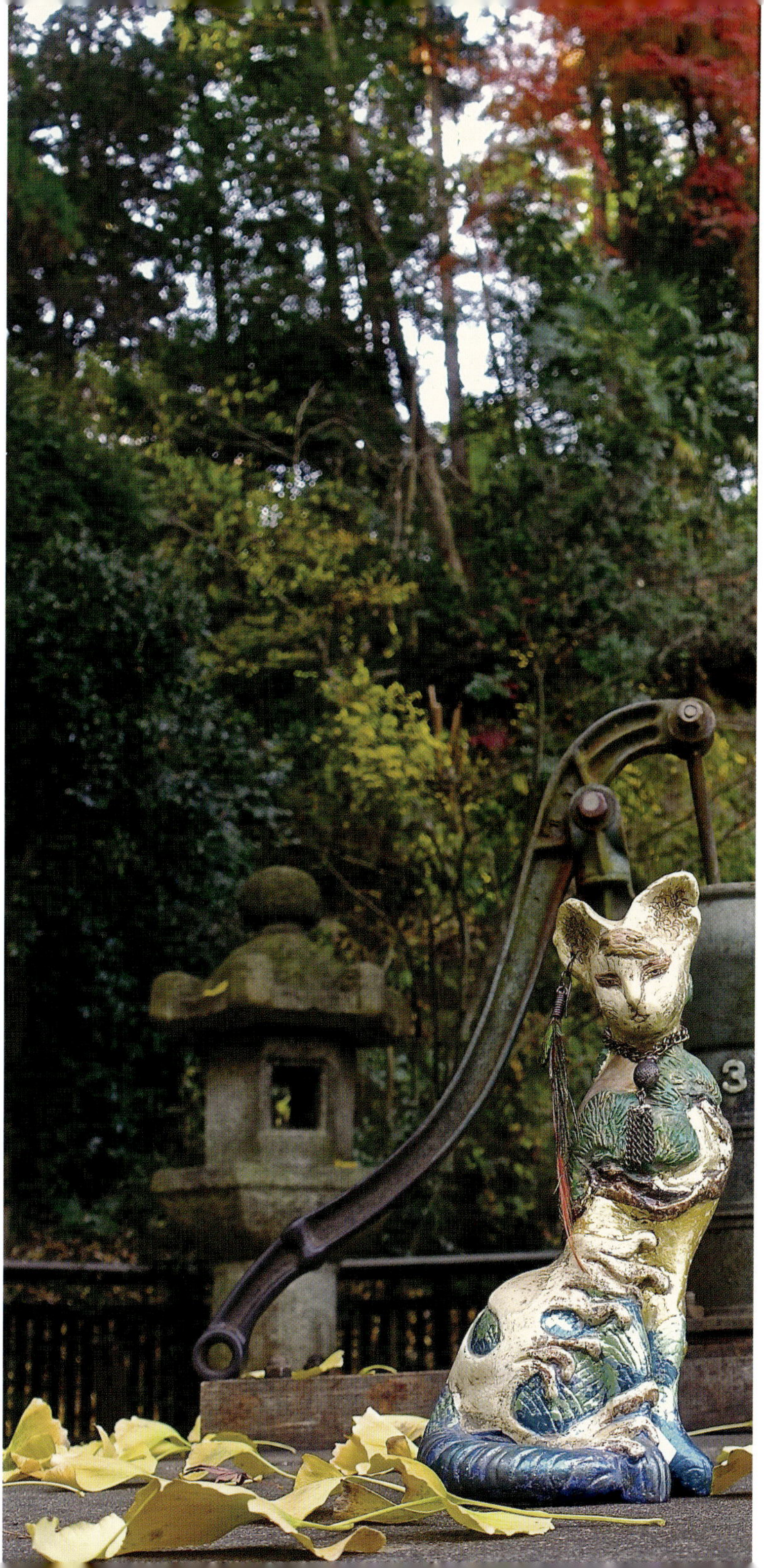

第十五帖 蓬生(よもぎふ)

尋ねても われこそは訪はめ 道もなく 深き蓬の もとの心を　源氏
(自分で草を分け尋ねよう。通う道もないくらい深い蓬の宿の、昔にかわらぬ姫君の心を)

故常陸宮の姫君・末摘花は、訪れる人もなく荒れ果てていく邸で暮らしていました。源氏はたまたまその邸の前を通りかかり、ようやく末摘花を思い出して再会しました。そして、蓬の生い茂る中で自分をひたすら待ち続けた末摘花に感動してわが疎遠を悔い末永い庇護を誓うのでした。

Chapter 15 Yomogiu (Wormwood)

[Genji] Tazunete mo / Ware koso towame / Michi mo naku / Fukaki yomogi no / Moto no kokoro o
(I will plow my way through grasses to find the heart of Princess at the deep of wormwood without a track to follow.)

Daughter of late Hitachi-no-miya, Suetsumuhana lived in her mansion that is running down without anyone visiting her.
When Genji passes by the mansion by chance, he recalls Suetsumuhana and meets her again. Impressed by her waiting for him patiently in the garden overrun by wormwood, he repents for the alienation and makes a pledge to take her under his wing forever.

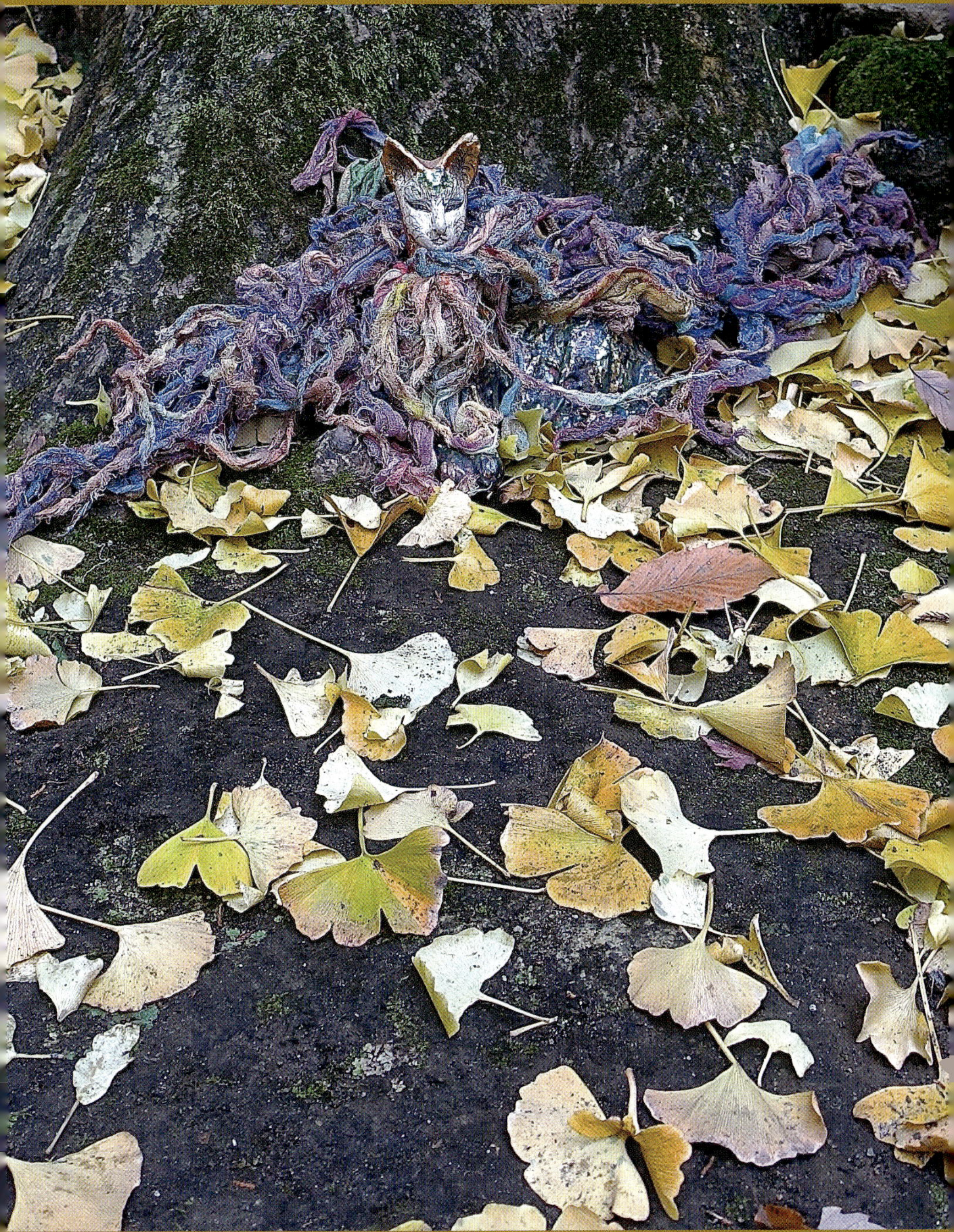

Chapter 16 Sekiya (Gatehouse)

[Utsusemi] Ausaka no / Seki ya ikanaru / Seki nare ba / Shigeki nageki no / Naka o wakuran
(The name of this gatehouse, Ausaka, is the homonym of "encounter", but why does it cause lament and separate people?)

Utsusemi has been sent to the eastern district with her husband who was assigned new work there.
At the Ausaka gatehouse on her way back to Kyoto after the term of office of her husband, she met by chance the gorgeous party of Genji who is going to visit the Ishiyama temple.
Genji feels nostalgia and sends her a letter. Reading it, Utsusemi reminds the old days and feels deep attachment to them.

第十六帖 関谷(せきや)

逢坂の関や いかなる関なれば しげき嘆きの 中を分くらむ 空蟬

(逢うと言う名の逢坂の関とは、どういう関所ゆえに、こうも深い嘆きを重ねるのでしょう)

空蟬は、夫の赴任に伴い東国に下っていました。任期終了で上京のため逢坂の関にさしかかった時、石山詣でに出向く豪勢な源氏一行に偶然出会います。

源氏は懐かしく思い空蟬に手紙を送り、彼女はそれに昔日を思い、感慨にふけるのでした。

第十七帖　絵合 （ゑあはせ）

大臣参りたまひて「同じくは、御前にてこの勝負定めむ」とのたまひなりぬ（源氏の大臣が参内なさって、「同じ事なら、帝の御前でこの勝負を定めよう」とおっしゃることになった）

源氏が後見になった故六条御息所の娘は、冷泉帝に入内して梅壺女御になりました。絵画を好む冷泉帝は、絵に堪能な梅壺の女御に次第に惹きつけられてゆき、既に入内していた弘徽殿女御の父・権中納言は帝の関心を引き戻そうと、当代有数の絵師を集め贅を尽くして絵画を制作させます。源氏達も秘蔵の絵画を取りそろえるなどして、双方の競争は白熱化してゆき、帝の御前で臨席者も判者も素晴らしい方達の、宮中を挙げて盛大な絵合わせが行われました。

Chapter 17　E-Awase (Picture Contest)

Ooomi Mairi-tamaite … onajiku ha gozen nite kono shobu sadamenu to notamai-tamamu
(Minister Genji comes to the court and is interested in the contest of pictures. He said, "The issue of this contest is better be decided in the presence of the Emperor".)

The daughter of Lady Rokujō Miyasu-dokoro for whom Genji acts as a guardian enters into the palace of Emperor Reizei and becomes Lady Umetsubo-no-nyōgo.
Emperor Reizei who is known to be a great amateur of pictorial art begins to be attracted by Umetsubo-no-nyōgo who is good at drawing pictures.
Emperor Reizei already has Kokiden-nyōgo as a concubine. Knowing the change of mind of the Emperor, her father who is a Gon-chunagon gathers famous painters to have them produce lavish pictures in order to attract the interest of the Emperor toward his daughter again. So Genji and his company also started to prepare their treasured paintings to compete with them. The competition gets so heated that a great contest of pictures is held in the presence of the Emperor by participation of the most excellent competitors and judges of the time.

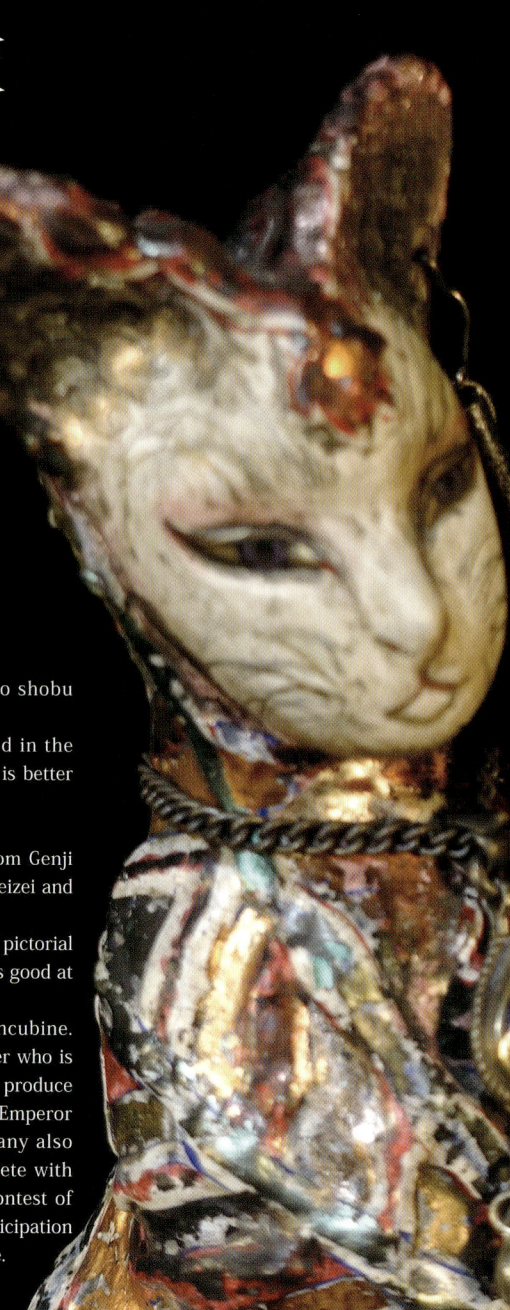

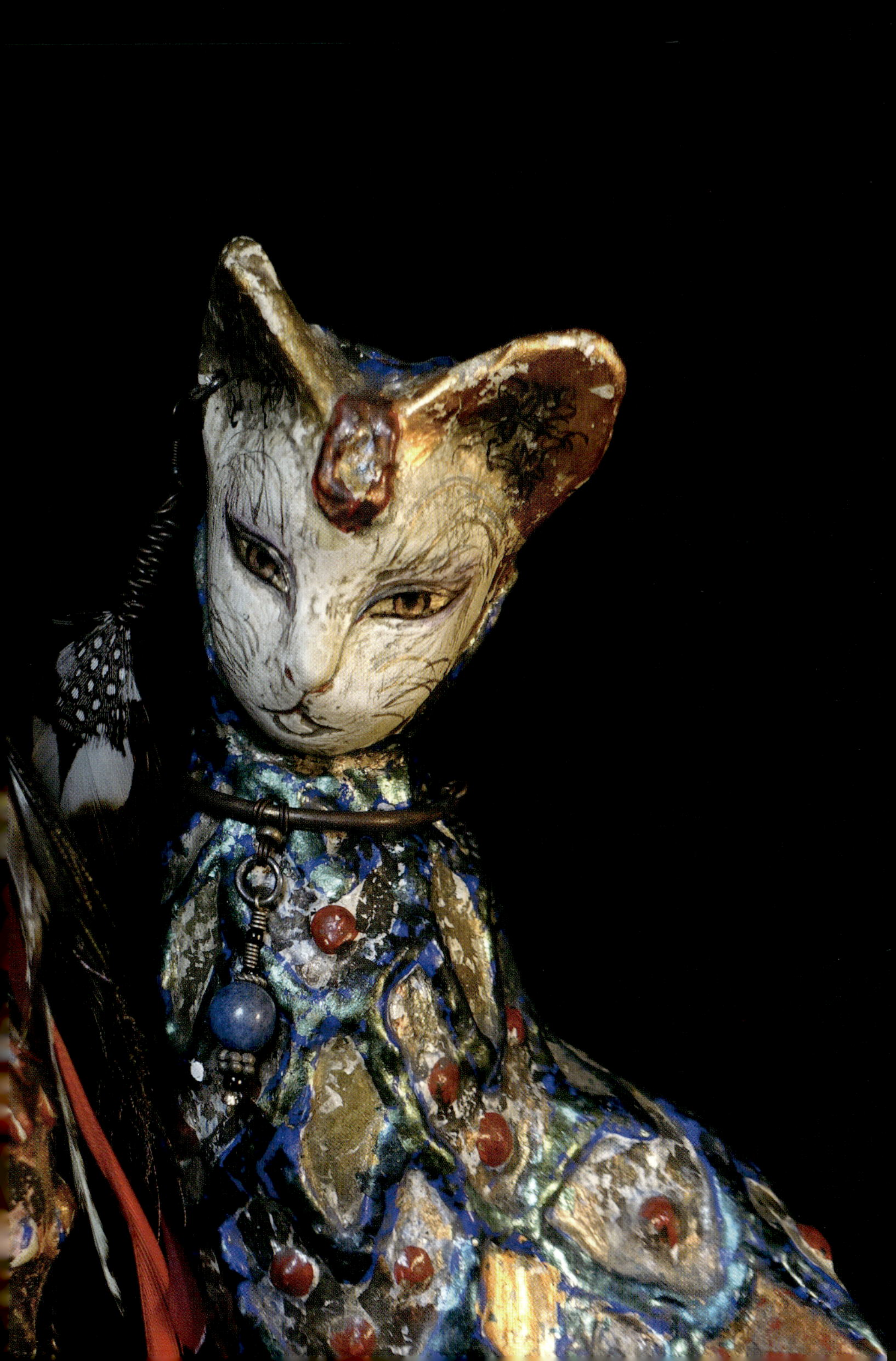

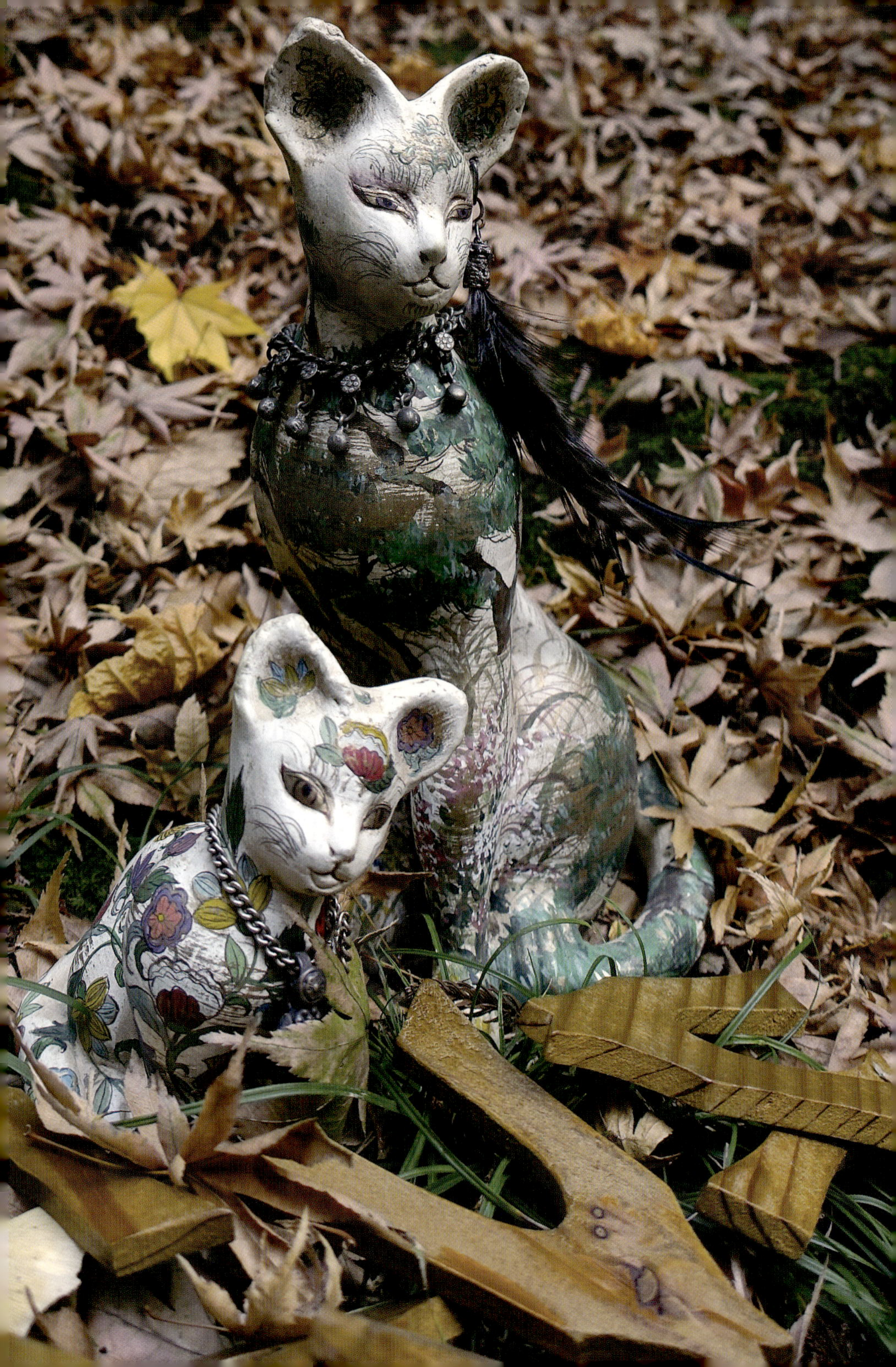

第十八帖　松風(まつかぜ)

変わらじと　契しことを　頼みにて　松のひびきに　音を添へしかな　　明石の君

（お約束を頼みとして、松の響きに泣く音を添えて、お待ちしておりました）

ふる里に見し世の友を恋ひわびてさへづることを誰かわくらん　　明石の君

（故郷恋しさに弾く琴の音を、誰が聞き分けてくれるでしょう）

　源氏の催促で明石の君は、姫君、母尼君とともに密かに上京し、大堰の邸に落ち着きました。
　明石の浦を思わせる大堰の景色は、懐かしい故郷をあとにしてきた母子の感慨深く、琴の響きに調子を合わせる松風も、どこか明石の地に似て郷愁を誘います。
　源氏は、初めて会う幼い姫君が予想以上に愛らしく、自邸への引取りを思案します。

Chapter 18　Matsukaze (Wind Blowing through Pines)

[Akashi-no-kimi] Kawaraji to / chigirishi koto o /Tanomi nite / Matsu no hibiki ni / Ne o soeshi kana
(Trusting in your promise, I have been waiting for you by adding by adding weeping music to the sighs of pine trees.)

[Akashi-no-kimi] Furusato ni / Mishi yo no tomo o / Koiwabite / Saedzuru koto o / Dareka wakuran
(Who would understand my heart from the sound of the harp I play with an ache for my native land?)

Urged by Genji, Lady Akashi secretly comes to Kyoto with her daughter and mother, and settles themselves in a house in Ōzeki.
The landscape of Ōzeki which resembles that of the Akashi-no-ura Sea arouses deep feelings to the mother and daughter who has left their home.
The winds blowing through the pine trees sound as if they accompany the harp she plays, and induces nostalgia to the life in Akashi.
Genji finds that the daughter born between him and Lady Akashi is much more lovely than expected and considers to take her in his palace.

第十九帖　薄雲（うすぐも）

入日さす　峰にたなびく　薄雲は　もの思ふ袖に　色やまがへる　源氏

（夕日の射す峰にたなびく薄雲は、悲嘆に暮れている私の喪服の袖に色を似せているのだろうか）

天変地異が頻発する年の春、源氏の愛する藤壺の女院が崩御しました。源氏は人に怪しまれぬよう念誦堂に籠り、一日中泣いて暮らしました。悲しみで何一つ見えないのに、夕日がはなやかに射して、山際に雲が薄く鈍色にたなびくのが、しみじみと目に入ります。

Chapter 19　Usugumo (Thin Cloud)

[Genji] Irihi sasu / Mine ni tanabiku / Usugumo wa / Mono omou sode ni / Iro ya magaeru
(The colour of the thin cloud drifting above the peak shined by the setting sun resembles the colour of the sleeves of the mourning wear I wear in grief.)

In the spring of a year with frequent extraordinary natural phenomena, Lady Fujitsubo passed away.
Grieving at the death of the lady he loves. Genji shuts himself in a chapel so as not to arouse suspicion of others, and spent the days weeping.
Though he feels his grief makes him almost blind, the view of the setting sun shining brightly on a mountain and a thin cloud in a dull colour floating near the peak hit his eyes keenly.

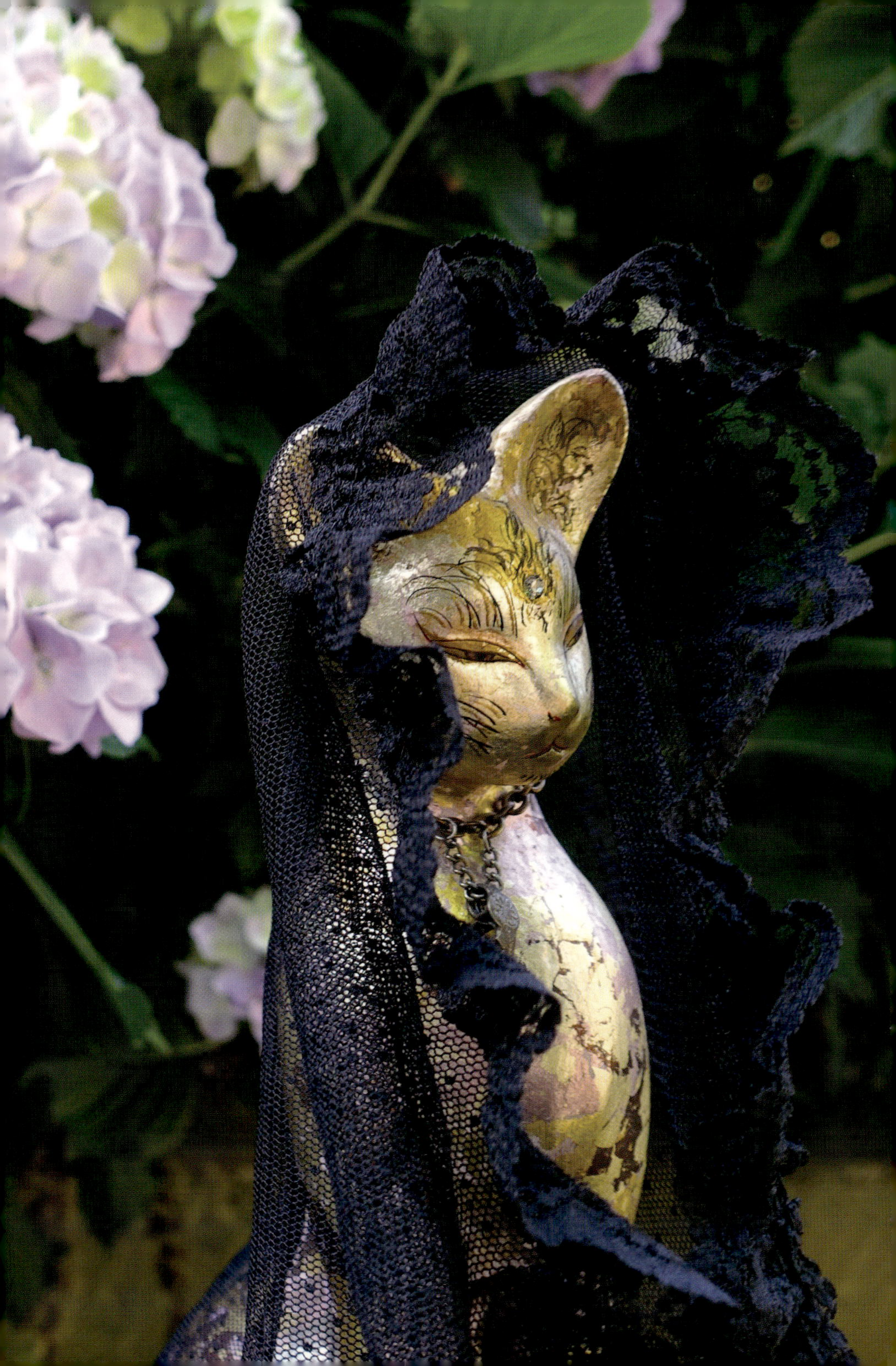

第二十帖 朝顔(あさがほ)

みしおりの つゆわすられぬ 朝顔の 花のさかりは 過ぎやしぬらん　源氏
(昔お目にかかった時のことが今もって少しも忘れられない花の盛り―あなたの盛りの美しさは過ぎておしまいになったのでしょうか)

秋果てて 霧の籬に むすぼほれ あるかなきかに うつる朝顔　朝顔の斎院
(秋の末、霧のかかった籬(まがき)に咲き残る朝顔のように、あるかなきかのはかない私です)

父・桃園卿の薨去により、朝顔の姫君は斎院を退き父宮の屋敷に移り住んでいました。以前からこの従妹の姫君に想いを寄せていた源氏は、叔母のお見舞いを口実に桃園邸にたびたび通いますが、姫君はつれないばかりです。
そのつれなさに想いが増す源氏は、ある日庭の朝顔と共に歌を送ります。

Chapter 20　Asagao (Morning Glory)

[Genji] Mishiori no / Tsuyu wasurarenu / Asagao no /Hana no sakari wa / Sugiyashinuran
(I can never forget you since I had an honour of seeing you in the bloom. Has that beautiful thing already gone?)

[Asagao-no-saiin] Aki hate te / Kiri no magaki ni / Musubōre / Aru ka naki ka ni / Utsuru asagao
(Like a morning glory flower remaining on a mist-moistened bamboo fence in the end of autumn, I am a fragile creature who is almost fading.)

After the demise of her father Prince Momozono, Lady Asagao retires from the post of priestess and moves to the mansion of her dead father. Genji, who has a long affection for the lady who is his cousin, often visits her mansion with an excuse of visiting his aunt who was sick, but the princess kept a distance from him.
Her cold treatment results only in increasing Genji's thoughts for her. One day, he sends her a poem together with the flower of morning glory in his garden, and a poem is returned from her.

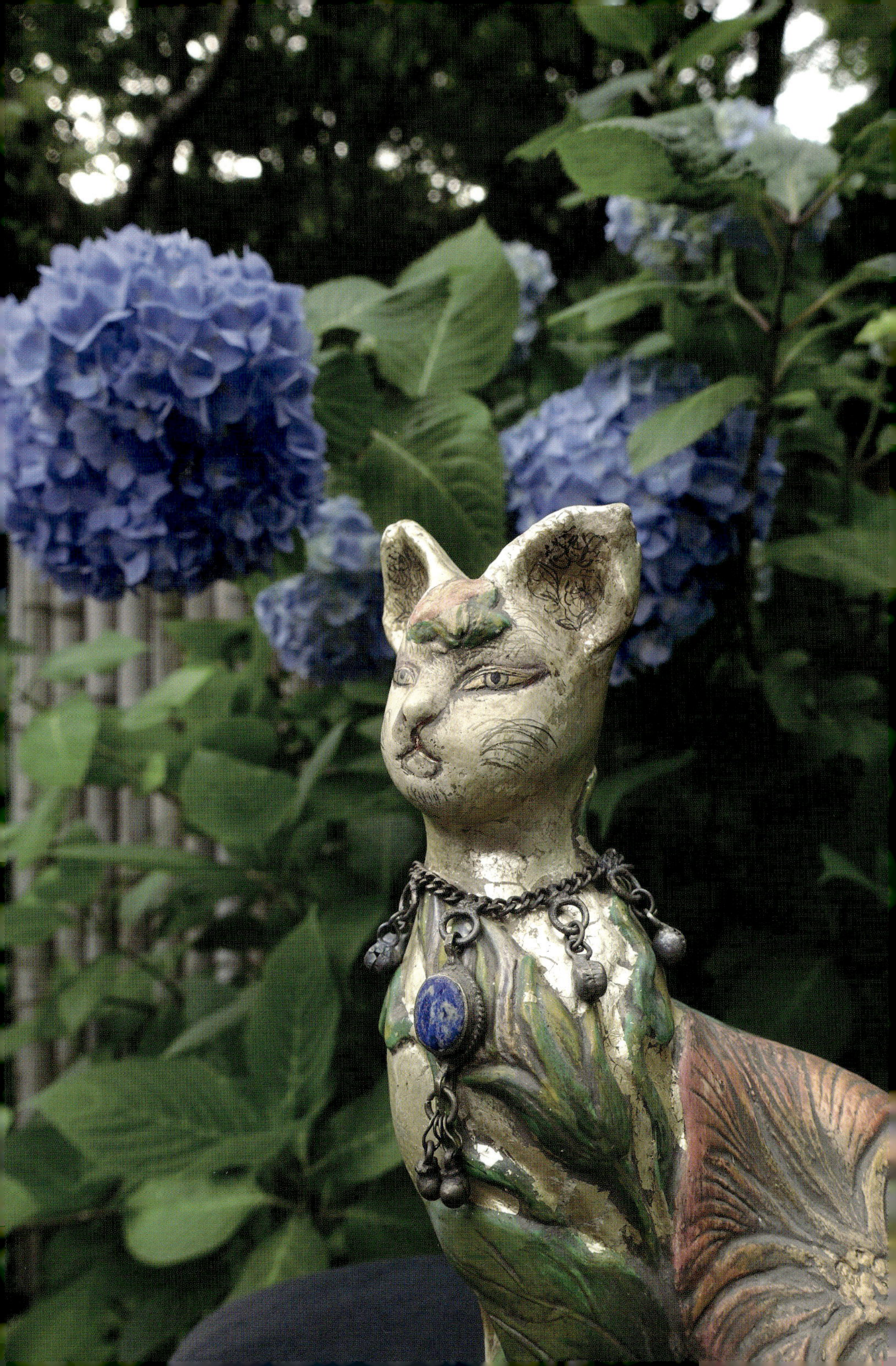

第二十一帖　少女(をとめ)

日かげにも　しるかりけめや　をとめごが　天の羽袖に　かけし心は　　夕霧
(あなたの五節の舞姿に思いをかけた心は、お分かりだったでしょう)

源氏の息子・夕霧は幼馴染の雲居の雁との恋仲を彼女の父に引離され、悲しみに打ちひしがれていました。その年の五節の舞姫(源氏の家臣・惟光の娘)に出会った夕霧は、雲居の雁の面影を求め、彼女に想いを寄せます。

Chapter 21　Otome (The Maiden)

[Yūgiri] Hikage ni mo / Shirukarikeme ya / Otomego ga / Ama no hasode ni / Kakeshi kokoro wa
(I wish you understand my heart clung on the maiden dancing with heavenly feathered sleeves.)

Genji's son, Yūgiri has been heartbroken since the love with Kumoi-no-kari, his childhood sweetheart, was torn apart by her father. In one of the seasonal festivals in the same year, Yūgiri finds a girl (daughter of Koremitsu who served Genji) who assumed the maiden dancers for the festival and begins to love her.

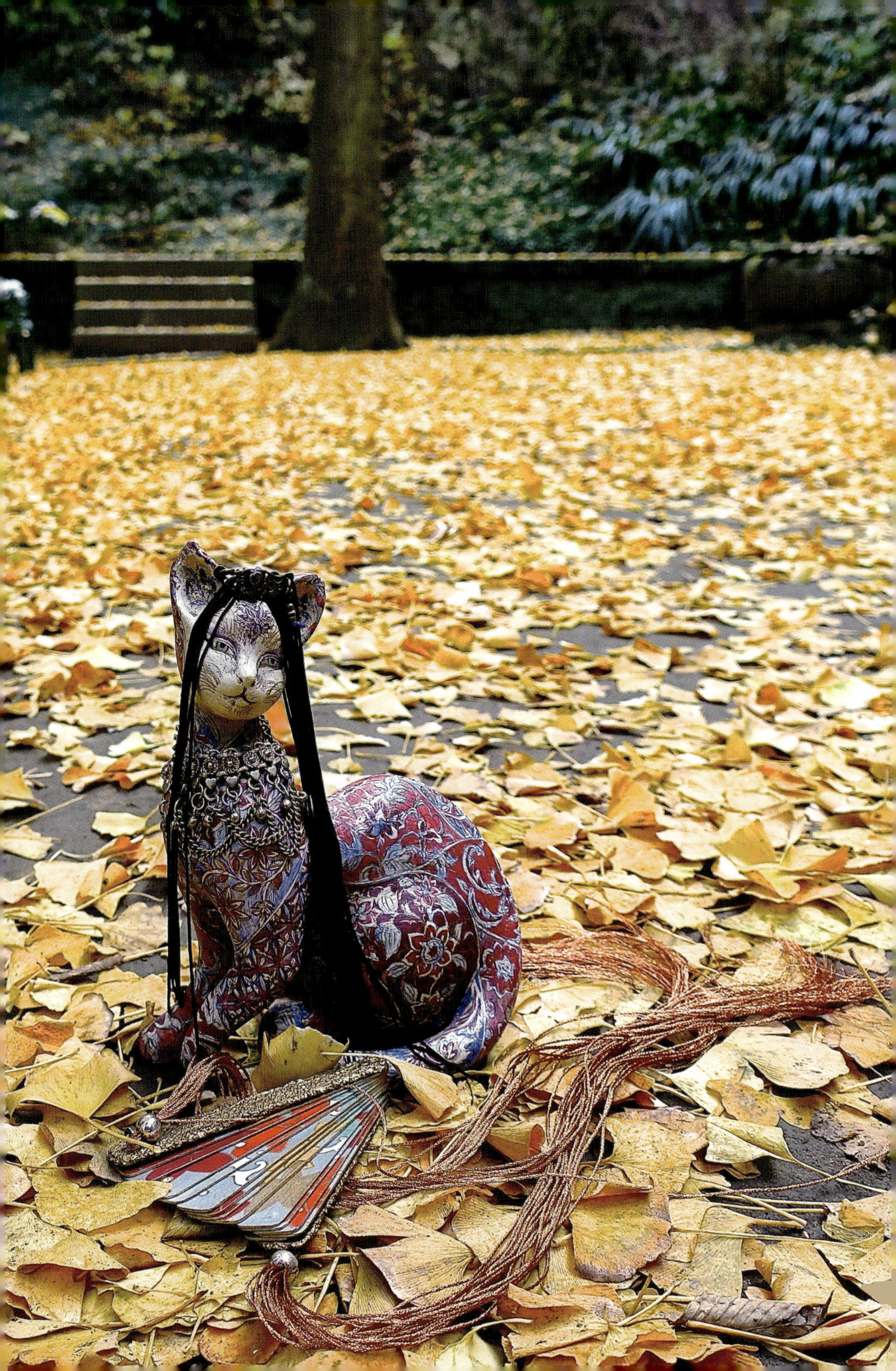

第二十二帖　玉鬘(たまかづら)

恋わたる 身はそれなれど 玉鬘 いかなる筋を 尋ね来つらむ　　源氏

（亡き夕顔を想い続けてきた自分の許に、その娘が来るようになるとはどのような縁であろう）

夕顔の遺児・玉鬘は乳母たちと肥前で暮らしていましたが、土地の豪族に無理やり結婚を迫られたために京に逃げてきました。そして父上に会えるようにとの初瀬参りで、偶然にかつての夕顔の侍女で今は源氏の女房の右近と巡り合います。

こうして玉鬘は源氏のもとに迎えられる事になりました。

Chapter 22　Tamakazura (Vine)

[Genji] Koiwataru / Mi wa sore naredo / Tamakazura / Ika naru suji o / Tazune kitsuran
(I am continuing to think of late I am continuing to think of late Yūgao, but what a lucky opportunity that her daughter happens to come to my house.)

The bereaved daughter of Yūgao, Tamakazura is living in Hizen together with her foster mother. However, as the local strong man tries to marry her by force, she runs to Kyoto. When she goes to Hase for praying for meeting her father, she by chance meets Ukon, who once was a maid to Yūgao and is presently working under Genji.
In this way, Tamakazura is received into Genji's palace.

53

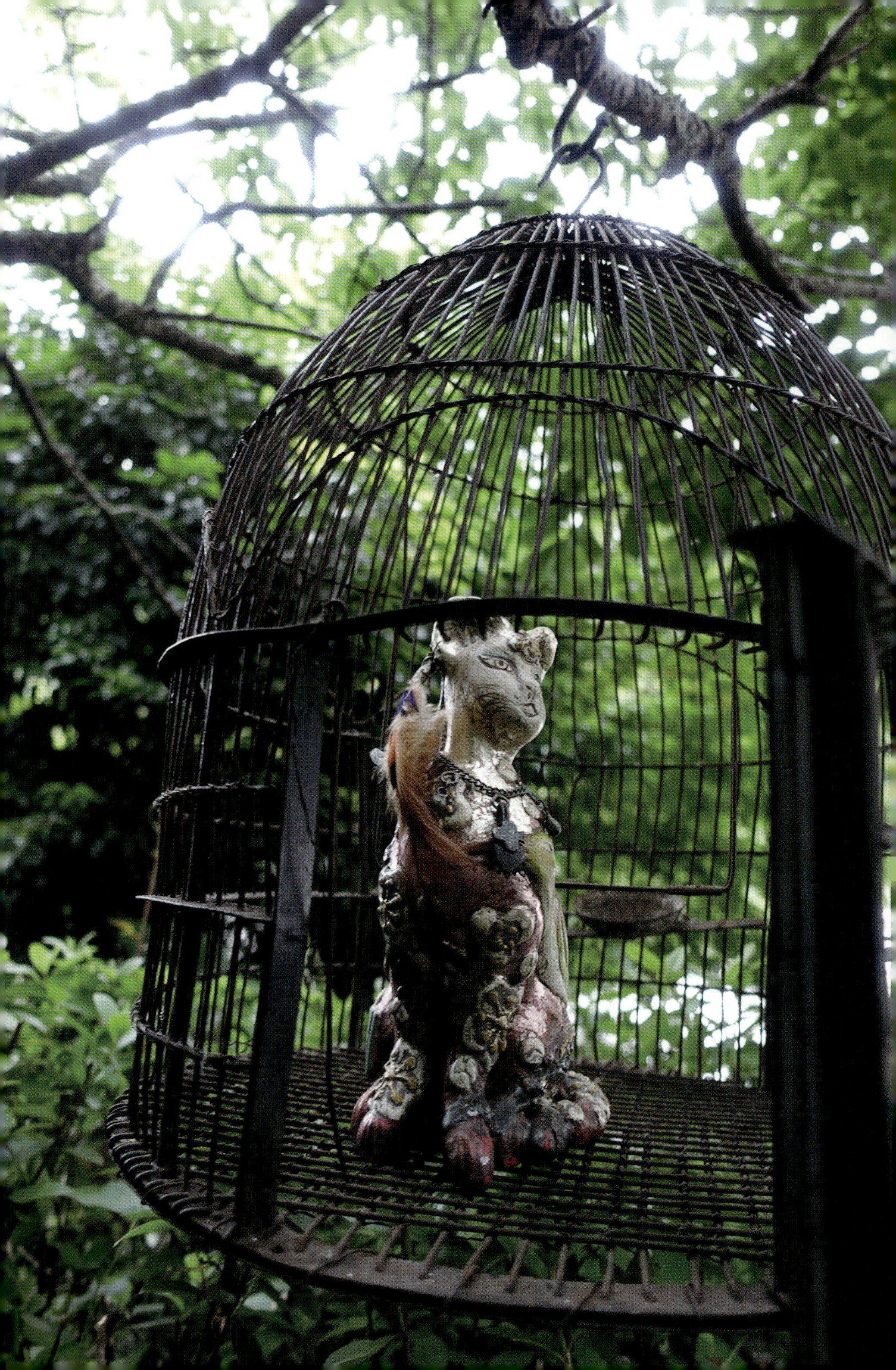

第二十三帖　初音 (はつね)

年月を　まつにひかれて　経る人に　今日鶯の　初音きかせよ　　　明石の君

　（長い年月ご成長を待ち焦がれている母に、初のお便りを下さいまし）

　　四季の町からなる源氏の新邸・六条院に初めての新年がやってきました。その素晴らしさはこの世の極楽のようです。
　　源氏は新年の挨拶に、そこに住む御方々のもとを訪れました。明石の君は離れて暮らしていた姫君に、新年のお祝いと一緒に文を届けます。

Chapter 23　Hatsune (Warbler's First Song)

[Akashi-no-kimi] Toshitsuki o / Matsu ni hikarete / Furu hito ni / Kyo uguisu no / Hatsune kikase yo
(Through long years and months, Mother has been waiting for her bush warbler's growth. Today permit me to listen to the first song of the year.)

The first near year has come to Rokujo-in, which is Genji's new palace
Composed of four houses representing the seasons, the splendid palace is almost like the paradise materialised in this world.
Genji visited the residents of his palace to say new year's greetings.
Lady Akashi sends a new year's gift and a letter to her daughter who lives separately from her.

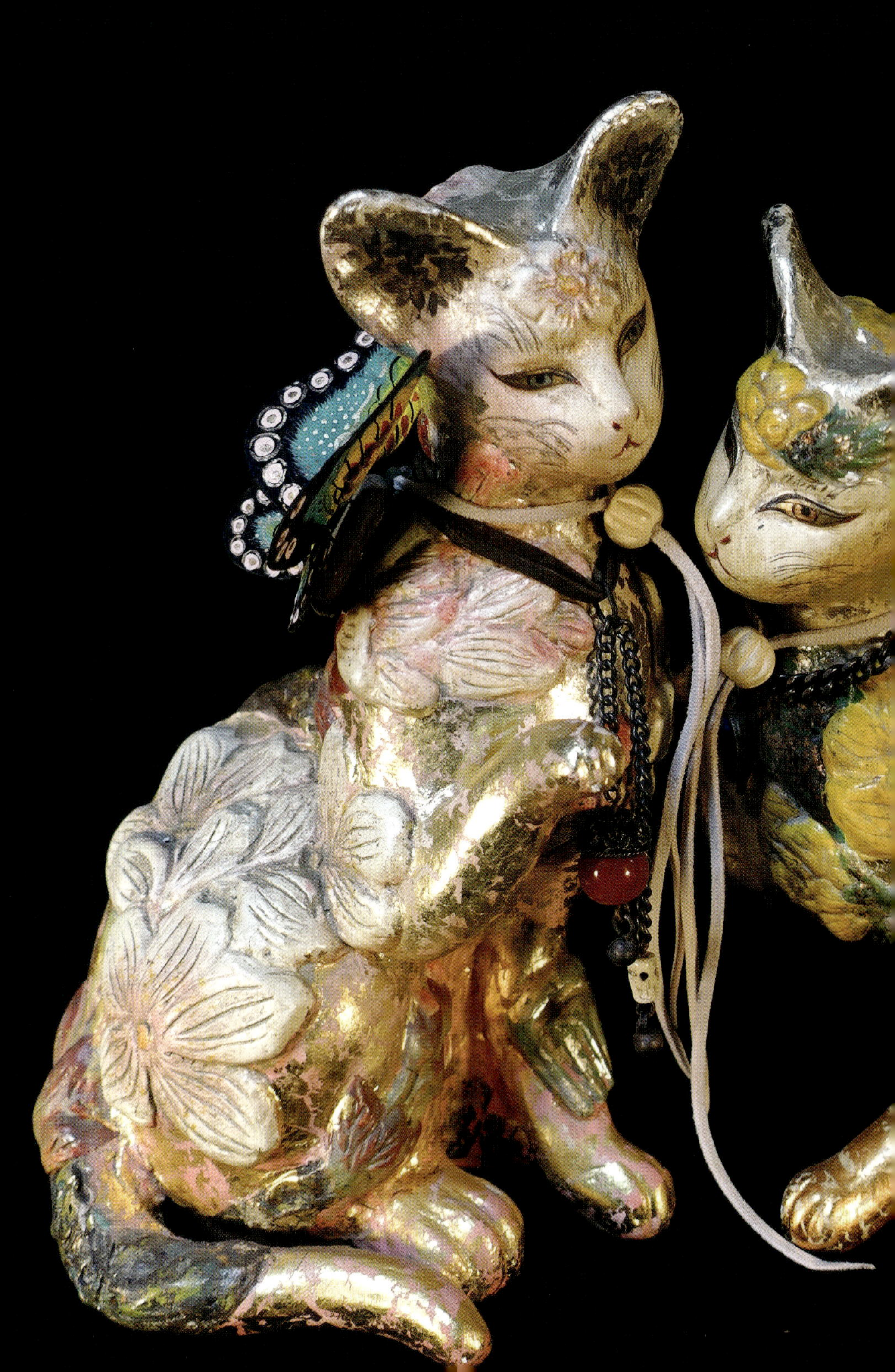

第二十四帖　胡蝶 (こてふ)

花園の　胡蝶をさへや　下草に　秋まつ虫は　うとく見るらむ　　紫の上

　　（春の園の胡蝶をさえ、秋をお好みのあなたにはお気に召さぬものとご覧になるでしょうか）

胡蝶にも　誘はれなまし　心ありて　八重山吹を　へだてざりせば　　秋好む中宮

　　（八重山吹の垣根の隔てがなければ、胡蝶に誘われて私もそちらに行きたかったのです）

　　　　　　　六条院で紫の上が住む春の町では、源氏が龍頭鷁首の船を浮かべ、優雅な船楽を催しました。翌日の秋好む中宮の御読経には、紫の上が鳥と蝶の衣装を着飾った女童達を使者に供物の花を贈り、秋好む中宮と歌を交わします。

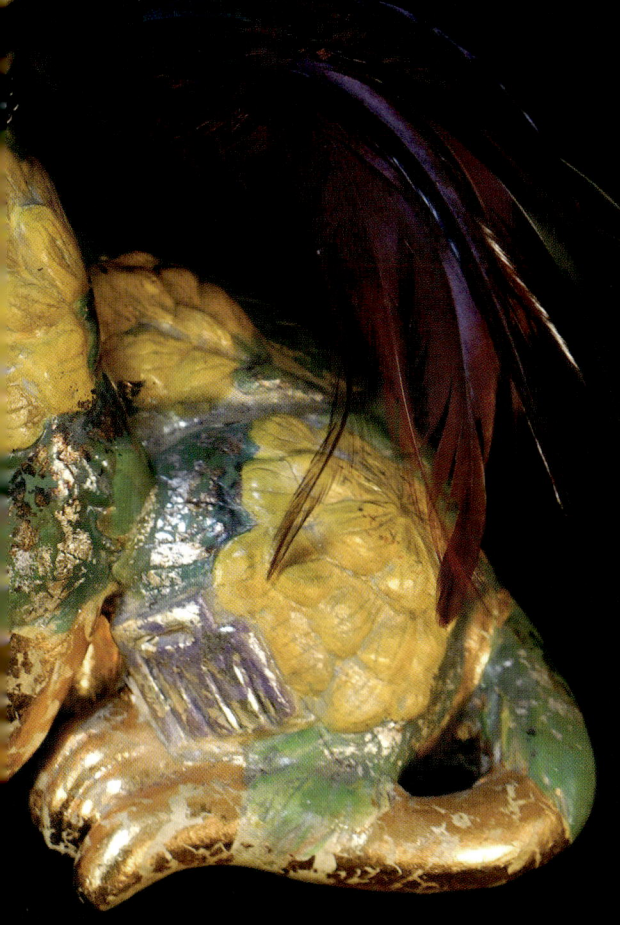

Chapter 24　Kochō (Butterflies)

[Murasaki-no-ue] Hanazono no / Kochō o sae ya / Shitakusa ni / Aki matsu mushi wa / Utoku muru ran
(Like a cricket living in undergrowth, you who like autumn may not like even butterflies in the spring garden.)

[Aki-Konomu-Chūgū] Kochō ni mo / Sasoware namashi / Kokoro ari te / Yae Yamabuki o / Hetate zari se ba
(If the fence of double-kerria did not separate us, I would visit you on the invitation of butterflies.)

In the Spring House in Rokujō-in where Murasaki-no-ue lives, Genji held an elegant music meeting by floating a couple of imperial boats on the pond. In the sutra recital by Lady Aki-Konomi-Chūgū on the next morning, Lady Murasaki-no-ue sent offerings carried by girls dressed up in clothing featuring birds and butterflies. The two ladies exchanged poems between them.

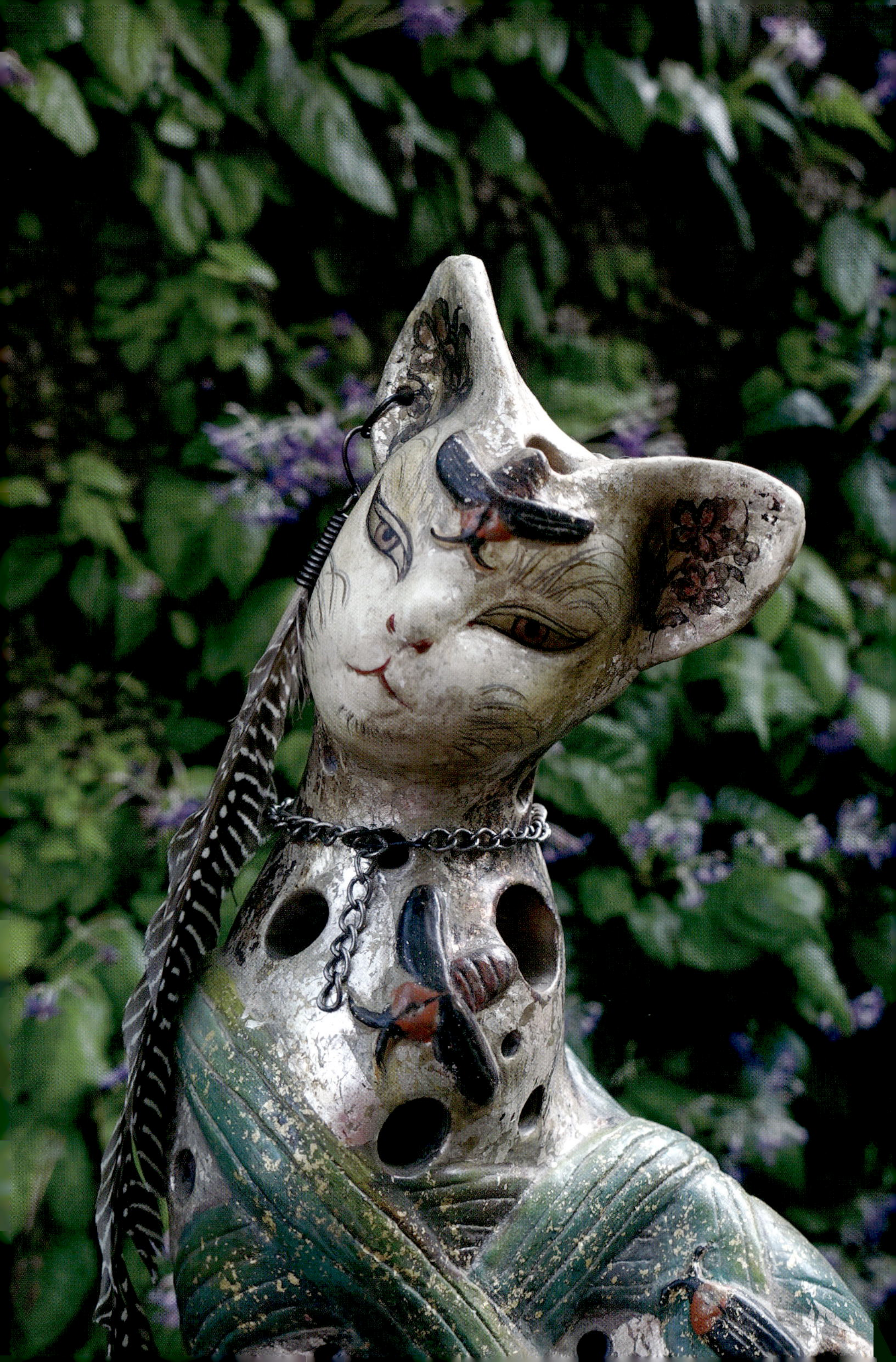

第二十五帖　蛍（ほたる）

なく声も　きこえぬ虫の　思ひだに
人の消つには　消ゆるものかは　　蛍兵部卿宮

（声のない蛍火さえも消せないものを、人の心の燃える想いが
どうして消せましょうか）

　　五月雨のある夜、蛍兵部卿宮は慕っている玉鬘のもとに
招かれます。源氏はその二人の対面の場に蛍の群れを放ち、
一瞬ほのかに照らし出される玉鬘の艶麗な姿に、宮の想いは
ますます募るのでした。

Chapter 25　Hotaru (Fireflies)

[Hotaru-Hyobukyo-no-Miya] Naku koe mo / Kikoenu mushi no / Omoi dani / Hito no ketsu ni wa / Kiyuru mono ka wa
(Even the glowing flame of voiceless fireflies cannot be extinguished, how can my burning hearts be extinguished?)

On a rainy night in early summer, Prince Hotaru-Hyobukyo-no-Miya is invited by Tamakazura he is longing for.
In the place of meeting of the two, Genji released a swarm of fireflies. Looking at the dazzling beauty of Tamakazura dimly illuminated in some moments, the love of the Prince grows stronger and stronger.

第二十六帖　常夏(とこなつ)

撫子の　とこなつかしき　色を見ば　もとの垣根を　人や尋ねむ　　源氏

　(忘れ形見のあなたの美しさを見たら、父君は母君のことをお尋ねになるでしょう)

いかでこの舌疾さやめはべらむ　近江の君

　(なんぞしてこの早口を治すことにいたしましょう)

源氏が「自分の娘」として引き取った玉鬘は美しく、とても評判が良い姫君でした。そこで内大臣(実は玉鬘の父)も娘を探し出してきましたが、引き取った近江の君は姿にも動作にも品が無く、早口で「内大臣の姫君」というには程遠い存在でした。

Chapter 26　Tokonatsu (Perpetual Summer)

[Genji] Nadeshiko no / Toko natsukashiki / Iro o miba / Moto no kakine o / Hito ya tazunen
(If your father sees how beautiful you are, he will ask about your mother.)

[Ōmi-no-kimi] Ikade kono shitadosa yamehaberamu
(How can I cure this fast mouth?)

Princess Tamakazura, who was received by Genji as his stepdaughter, is a very beautiful girl and has a high reputation among people... Naidaijin (actually the biological father of Tamakazura) imitates Genji and finds a stepdaughter. However, Ōmi-no-kimi he received is unrefined in both appearance and action. Speaking so fast, she is far from a presence deserving to be a "princess of Naidaijin".

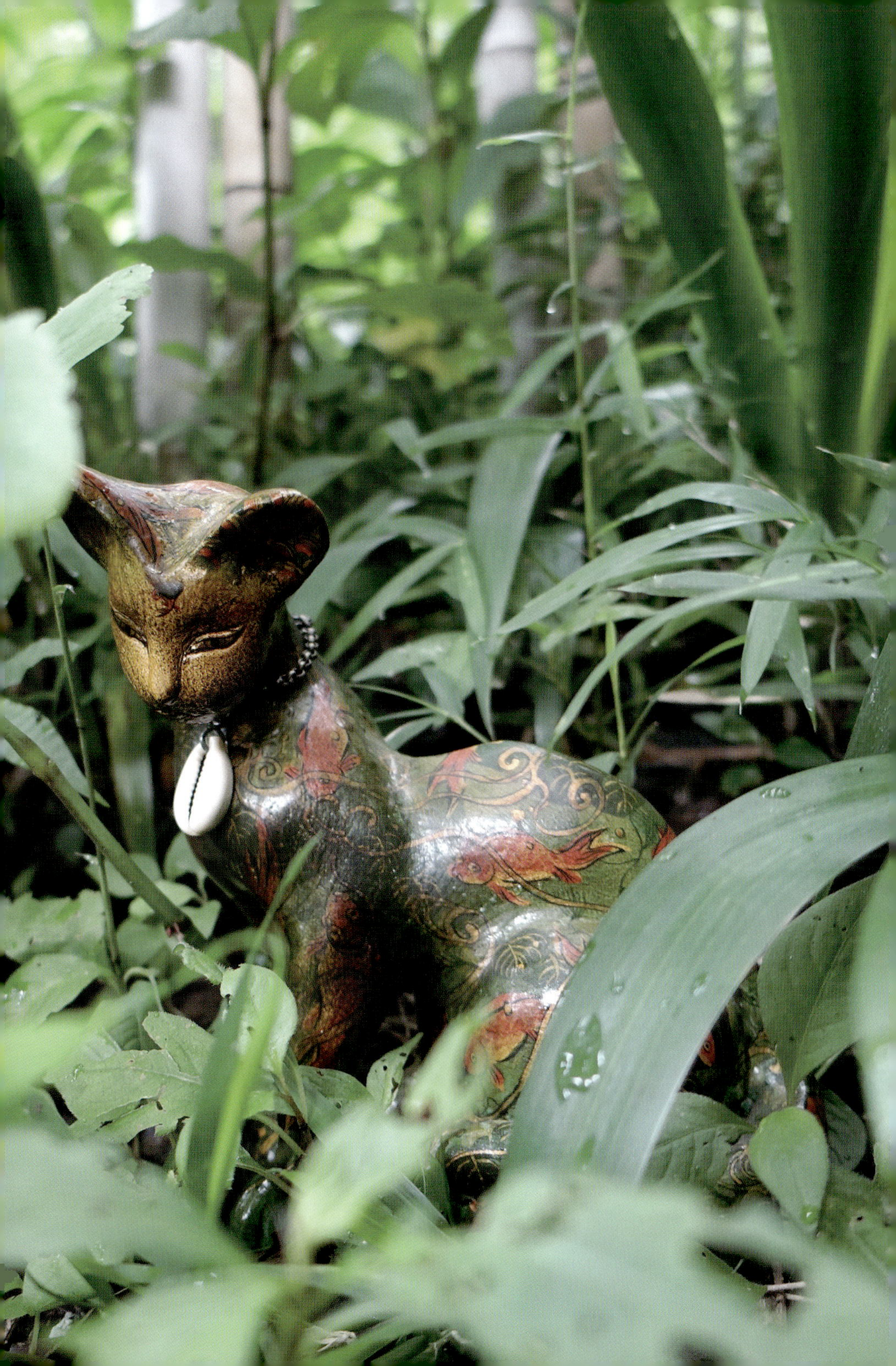

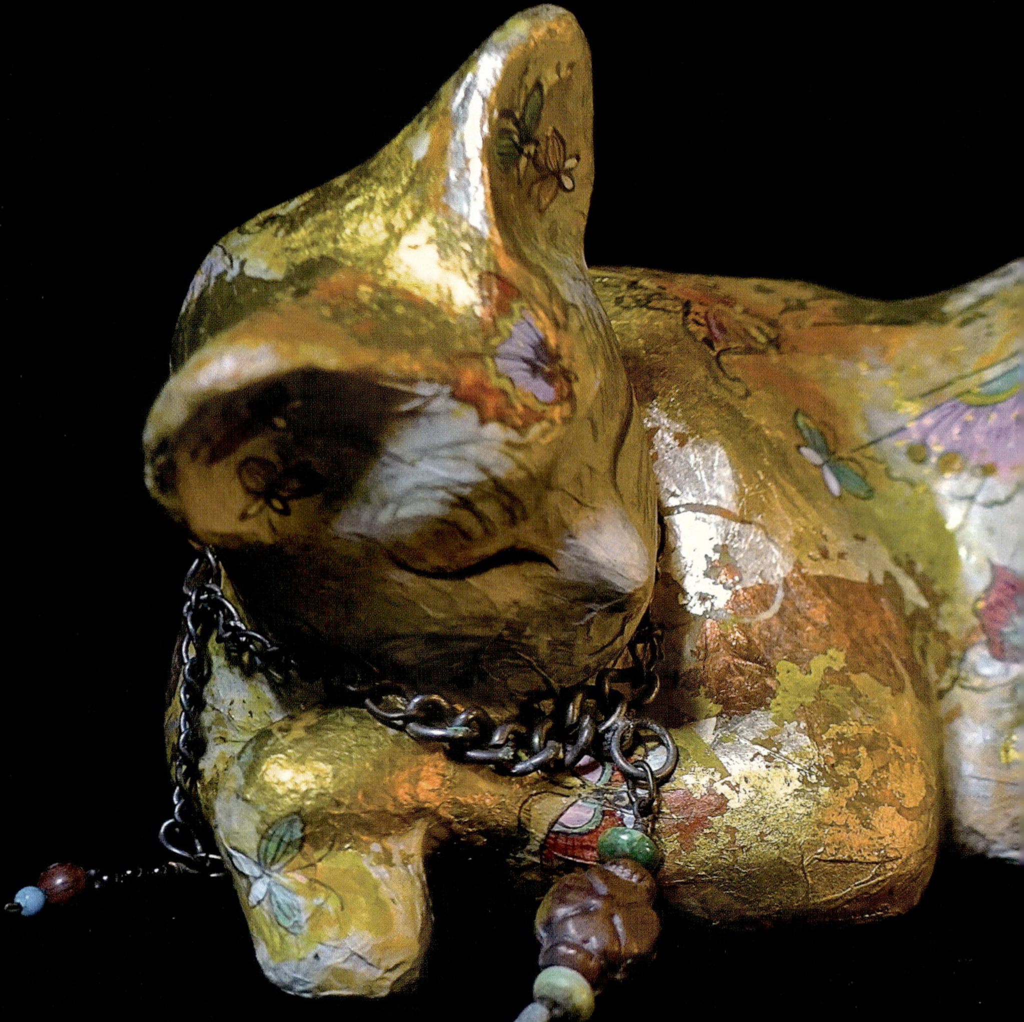

第二十七帖　篝火（かがりび）

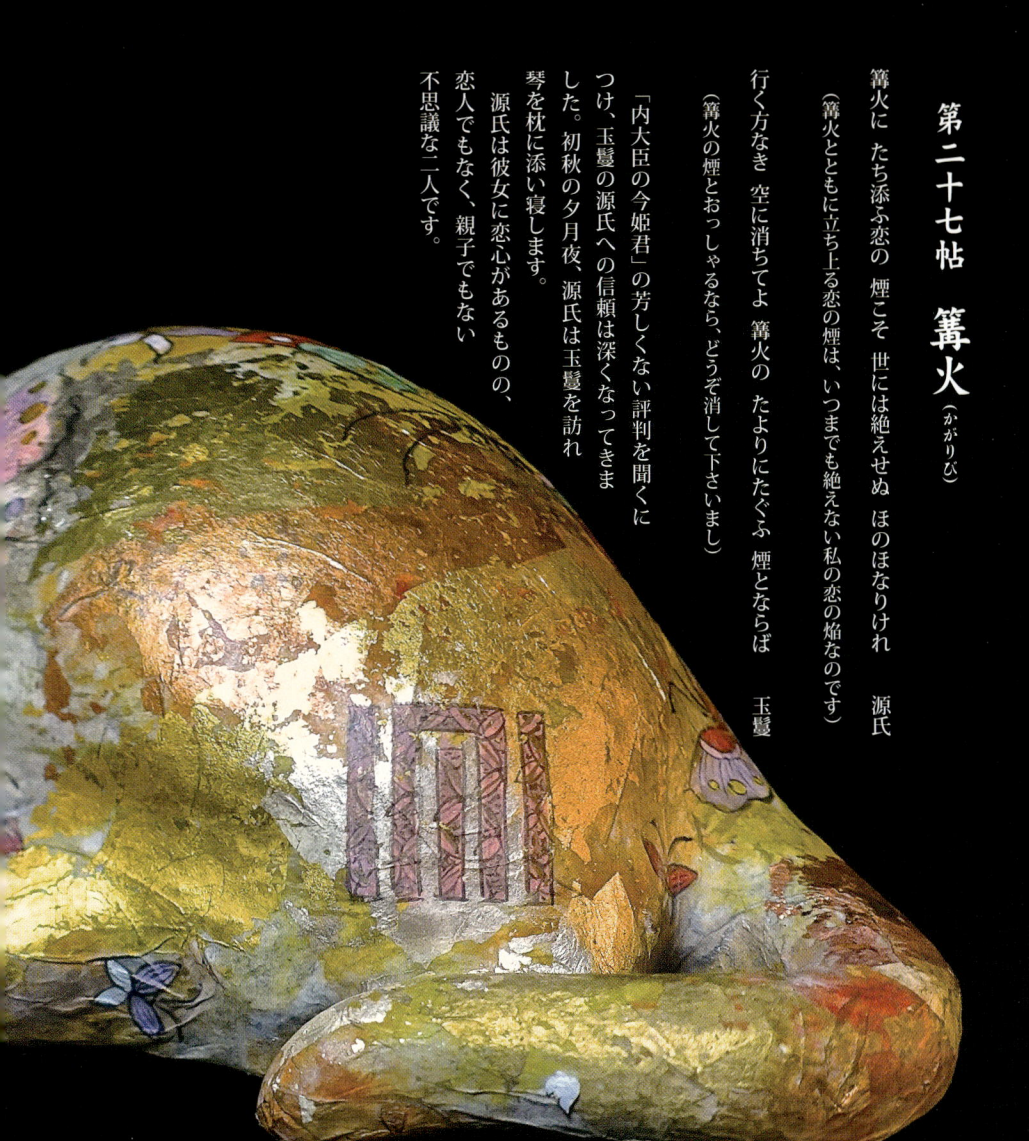

篝火に　たち添ふ恋の　煙こそ　世にには絶えせぬ　ほのほなりけれ　源氏
（篝火とともに立ち上る恋の煙は、いつまでも絶えない私の恋の焔なのです）

行く方なき　空に消ちてよ　篝火の　たよりにたぐふ　煙とならば　玉鬘
（篝火の煙とおっしゃるなら、どうぞ消して下さいまし）

「内大臣の今姫君」の芳しくない評判を聞くにつけ、玉鬘の源氏への信頼は深くなってきました。初秋の夕月夜、源氏は玉鬘を訪れ琴を枕に添い寝します。
源氏は彼女に恋心があるものの、恋人でもなく、親子でもない不思議な二人です。

Chapter 27　Kagaribi (Flares)

[Genji] Kagaribi ni / Tachisou koi no / Keburi koso / Yo ni ha taesenu / Honoo narikere
(The smoke of love rising from the flares comes from my flame of love that never ceases.)

[Tamakazura] Yukue naki / Sora ni kechite yo / Kagaribi no / Tayori ni taguu / Keburi to naraba
(Please let it vanish aimlessly in the sky if you say it is just the smoke of flares.)

Hearing the bad reputation of the "princess of Naidaijin", Tamakazura's confidence towards Genji has deepened further. On an evening with the moon in the sky, Genji visited Tamakazura and slept with his head on a koto.
Genji has come to love her, but the two remain in a strange relationship, being neither lovers nor a father and daughter.

第二十八帖 野分 (のわき)

さやうならむ人をこそ 同じくは見て明かし暮らさめ 夕霧
(あのような美しい人を妻に迎えて朝夕いっしょに暮してみたいもの)

例年にない激しい台風の日、夕霧は風の見舞いに訪れた六条院で、紫の上を垣間見てしまいます。父の源氏からは紫の上に近づく事を固く禁じられていたので、初めて目にする美しい人を見て、魂を奪われてしまいました。

Chapter 28 **Nowaki** (Typhoon)

[Yūgiri] Sayounaramu hito koso onajiku wa mite Akashi kurasame
(I wish to have such a beautiful woman as my wife and live together day and night.)

On a day of unusually severe typhoon, Yūgiri visits the Rokujō-in palace to check the palace and happens to glimpse Lady Murasaki-no-ue. As he is strictly forbidden by Genji to see her, his heart was stolen at the instant he sees the beautiful lady for the first time.

64

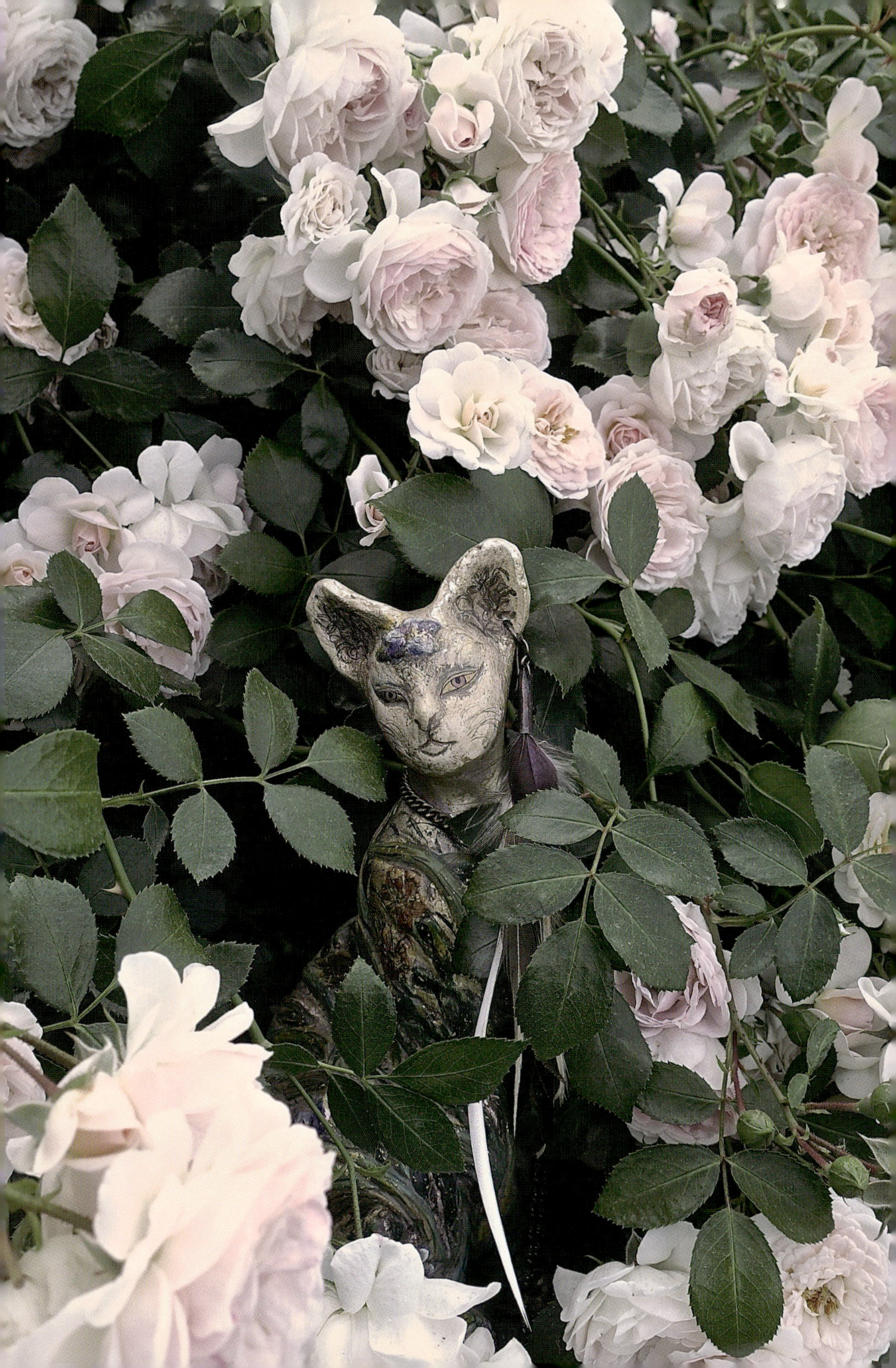

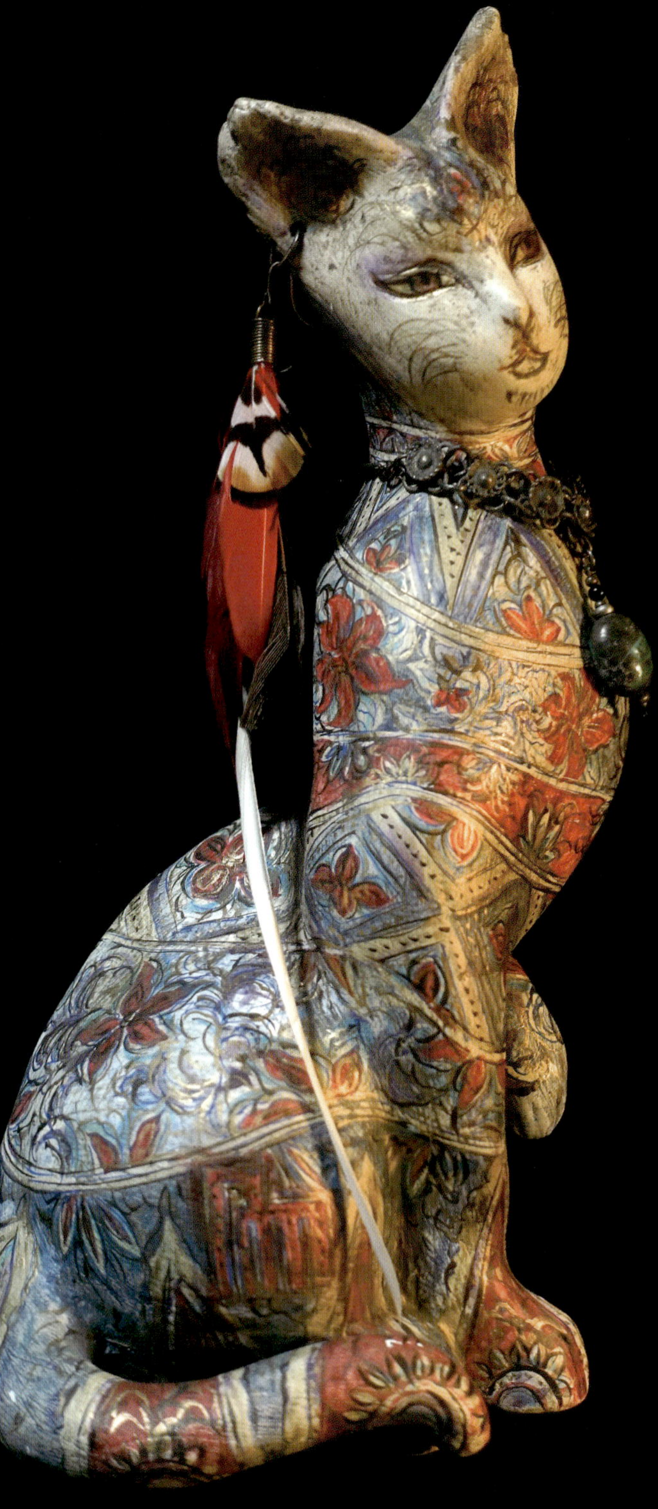

第二十九帖　行幸 (みゆき)

うちきらし 朝ぐもりせし みゆきには
さやかに空の 光やは見し　　玉鬘

（朝曇りの雪の日のことで、空の光（帝のお顔）もよく見られませんでした）

行幸（帝の外出）があり、その盛大な一行を見物に出た玉鬘は、初めて父・内大臣や求婚者達の姿を目にしました。中でも冷泉帝の美しさは特別で、かねて源氏の勧めていた宮中でのお仕事にも心が動くのでした。
　そして玉鬘の裳着の儀式に、初めて実父・内大臣と会います。

Chapter 29　Miyuki (Imperial Excursion)

[Tamakazura] Uchikirashi / Asagumori seshi / Miyuki ni wa / Sayaka ni sora no / Hikari ya wa mishi
(Because the excursion was under the cloudy morning sky on a snowy day, I could not see the light of the sky (Emperor) so clearly.)

On the day of Miyuki (Emperor's excursion), Tamakazura goes out to see the gorgeous party and notices her father and suitors for the first time.
Among them, the beauty of Emperor Reizei was exceptional, which makes her reconsider work in the Imperial Court recommended by Genji. In her coming-of-age celebration ceremony, she meets Naidaijin, her biological father, for the first time.

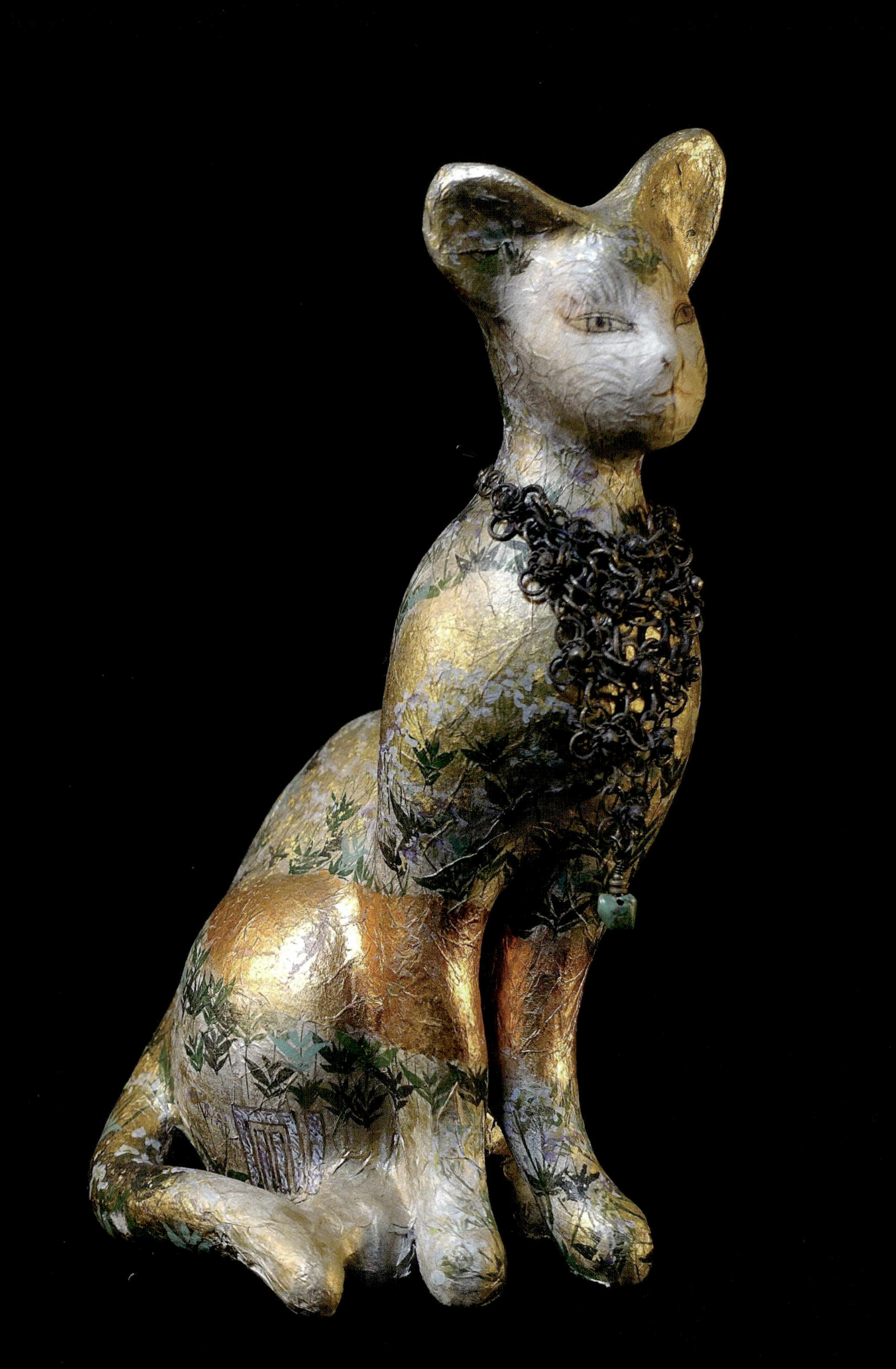

第三十帖　藤袴 (ふじばかま)

おなじ野の　露にやつるる　藤袴
あはれはかけよ　かごとばかりも　　夕霧

　　（同じ縁につながる私の恋を、少しでもあわれと思ってい下さい）

　玉鬘が内大臣の娘であり、宮仕えをすることが公になりました。
　夕霧は玉鬘を姉と思っていたのに遠縁とわかり、ある日藤袴の花を御簾の下から差し入れて、恋心を伝えました。

Chapter 30　Fujibakama (Thoroughwort)

[Yūgiri] Onaji no no / Tsuyu ni yatsururu / Fujibakama / Aware wa kake yo / Kagoto bakari mo
(I am a thoroughwort in purple trousers wasted by the dew from the field. Please feel pity, even small, for the love of me who am from the same field as you.)

It is made public that Tamakazura is actually a daughter of Naidaijin and that she is going to court service,
Finding that Tamakazura who he used to think as an elder sister was actually of much distant relation, Yūgiri communicates his love to her by sending flowers of thoroughwort through the bottom of a bamboo blind.

第三十一帖　真木柱 (まきばしら)

今はとて. 宿離れぬとも　馴れ来つる
真木の柱よ　我を忘るな　　真木柱の君

　（今日限りこの家を去りますが、真木の柱よ私を忘れない
　　で下さい）

　　不本意ながら髭黒の大将の妻となってしまった
玉鬘は周囲の人々と共に嘆きましたが、大将は玉鬘を
家に迎え入れる準備を始めます。
　　長女の真木柱の君は大将の家を去る時、家の柱の
割れ目に歌を差し込みました。

Chapter 31　Makibashira (Cypress Pillar)

[Makibashira-no-kimi] Ima wa tote / Yado hanarenu tomo / Narekitsuru / Maki no hashira wa / Ware o wasuru na
(I will leave this house today but, cypress pillar to whom I am attached so deeply, please do not forget me.)

Unwillingly becoming a wife of General Higekuro, Tamakazura deplores her fate with people surrounding her, but the General begins preparation for receiving her in his mansion.
Makibashira, a daughter of the General has to leave the mansion and inserts her poem into a crack on one of its cypress pillars.

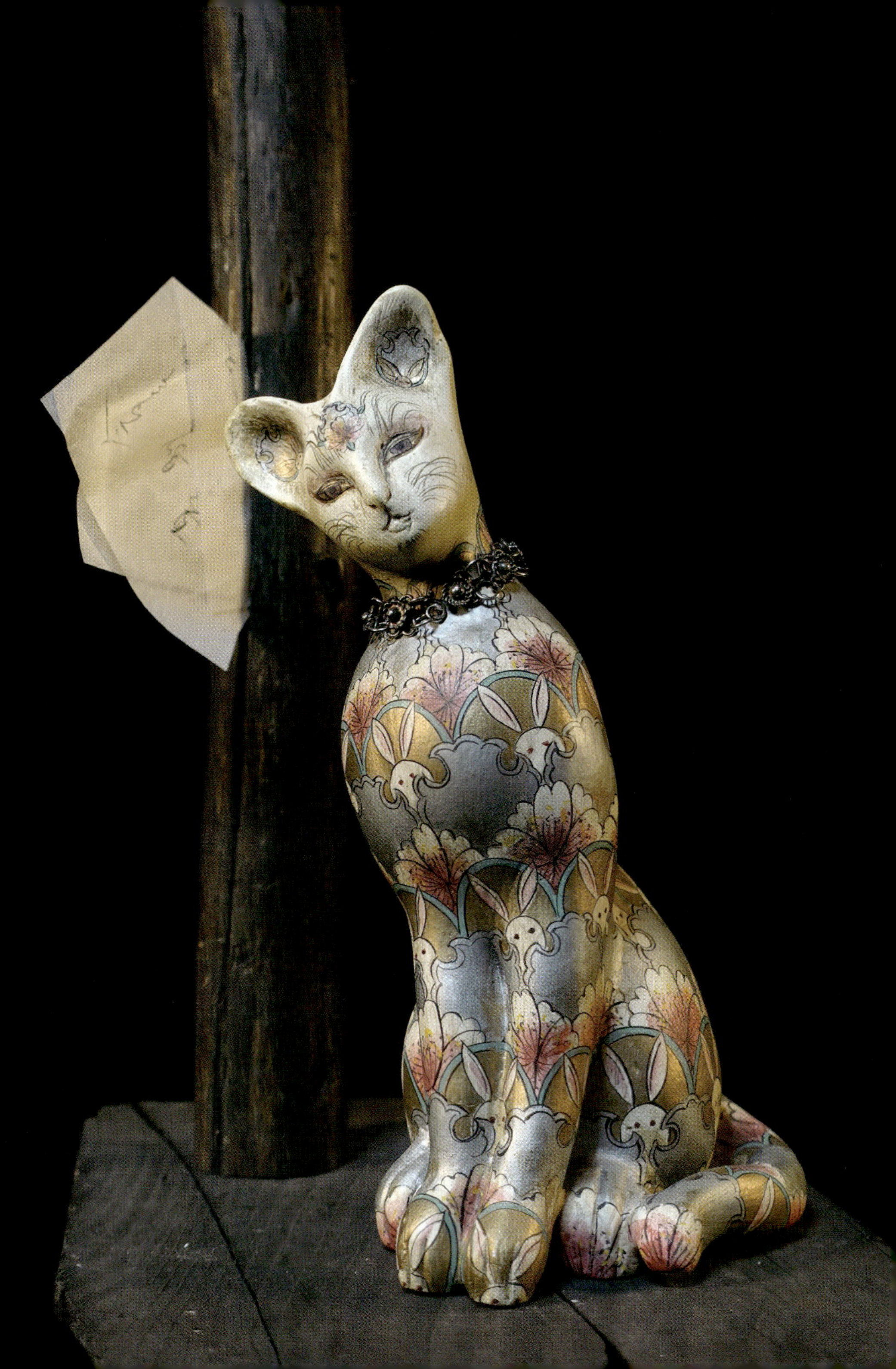

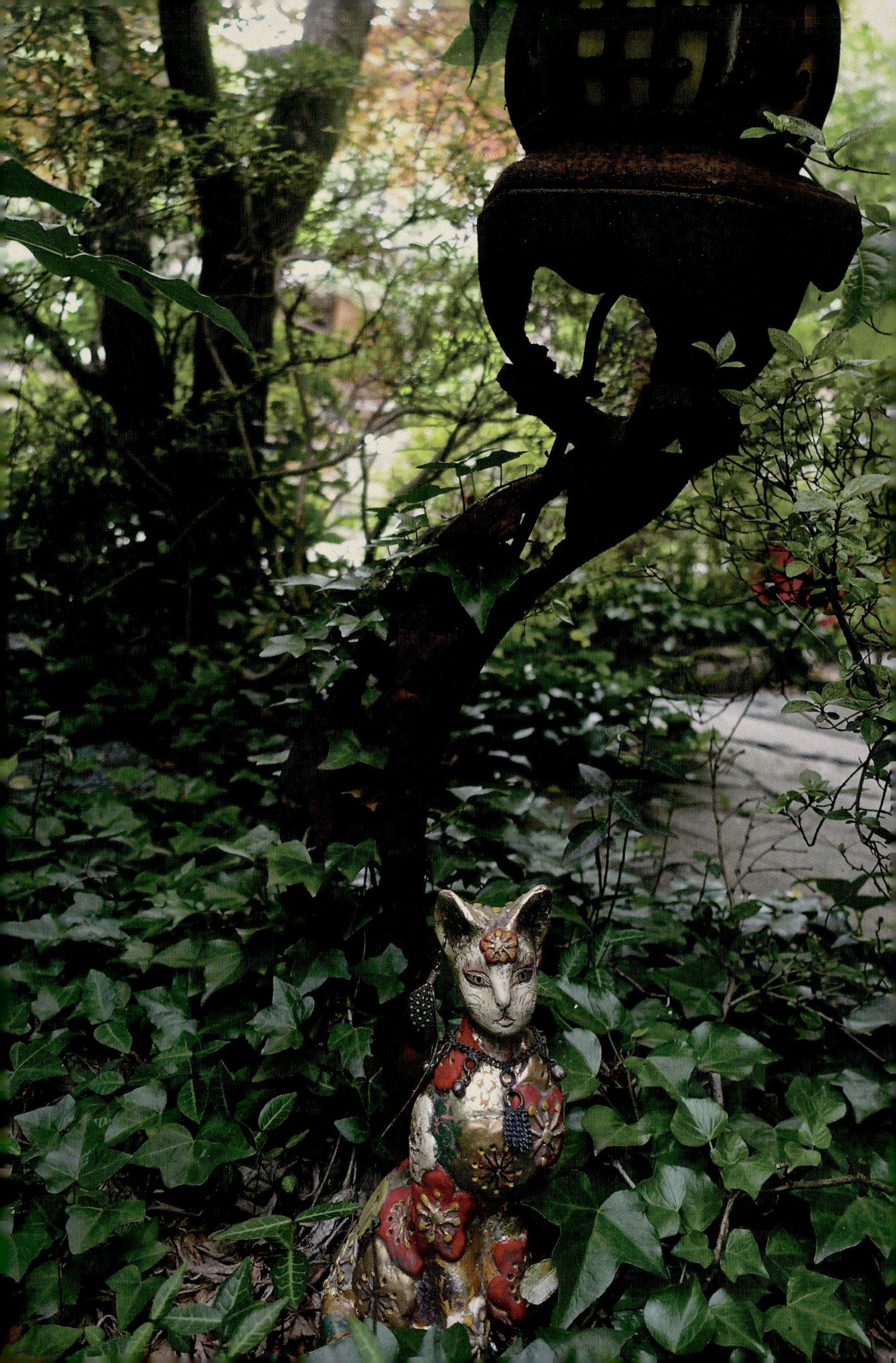

第三十二帖　梅枝（うめがえ）

梅が枝に　来ゐる鶯や　春かけて　はれ　春かけて　鳴けどもいまだや　雪は降りつつ
あはれ　そこよしや　雪は降りつつ　　　（催馬楽・梅が枝）

（梅の枝に来てとまっている鶯よ、冬から春にわたって、はれ
春にわたって鳴いているけれども、いまだによ、雪は降り続いていて
あはれ　そこよしや　雪は降り続いていて、春はまだ浅いことだ）

源氏は、明石の姫君の婚礼や裳着の儀を間近にして、様々な準備に忙しい日々です。
香も優れた方々に調合を依頼し、特別品が出来上がってきました。
そんな頃蛍兵部卿宮が訪れたので、薫物合わせを思い立ちました。

Chapter 32　Mume ga E (Palm Tree Branch)

[Mume ga E, ancient vocal court music] Mume ga E ni / Kiiru uguisu ya / Haru kakete hare / Haru kakete / Nakedomo imada ya / Yuki wa furitsutsu / Aware soko yoshi ya / Yuki wa furitsutsu
(The bush warbler on a plum tree branch sings from the winter throughout the spring, but the snow is still falling continuously. Here is the pathos of things. The snow is still falling while the spring has just come.)

As the wedding and coming-of-age celebration ceremony of his daughter approach, Genji is busy for various preparations. He ordered incenses to best experts and received custom-made ones. One day, Hotaru-Hyobukyo-no-Miya visits Genji. Genji thinks of doing an incense competition.

第三十三帖 藤の裏葉 (ふちのうらは)

春日さす 藤の裏葉の うらとけて 君し思はば 我も頼まむ 古歌より
(男が誠意を示してくれるのなら、こちらも心を開いてあてにしよう)

夕霧との和解を求めていた内大臣は、自邸の藤花の宴に夕霧を招待しました。それを察した源氏は、衣装にも気を配って夕霧を送り出します。そして夕霧は七年越しの恋を実らせて、内大臣の娘・雲居の雁と結婚しました。

Chapter 33
Fuji no Uraba (Wisteria Leaves)

[Old poem] Haruhi sasu / Fuji no uraba no / Ura tokete / Kimi shi omowaba / Ware mo tanoman (If you love me with a sincere mind, I will open my mind and trust in you.)

Seeking reconciliation with Yūgiri, Naidaijin invites him for the wisteria viewing party held in his mansion.
Genji understands his intentions and send Yūgiri to him in well-considered clothing.
This led Yūgiri to marry Kumoi-on-Kari, a daughter of Naidaijin, in the seventh year since he fell in love with her.

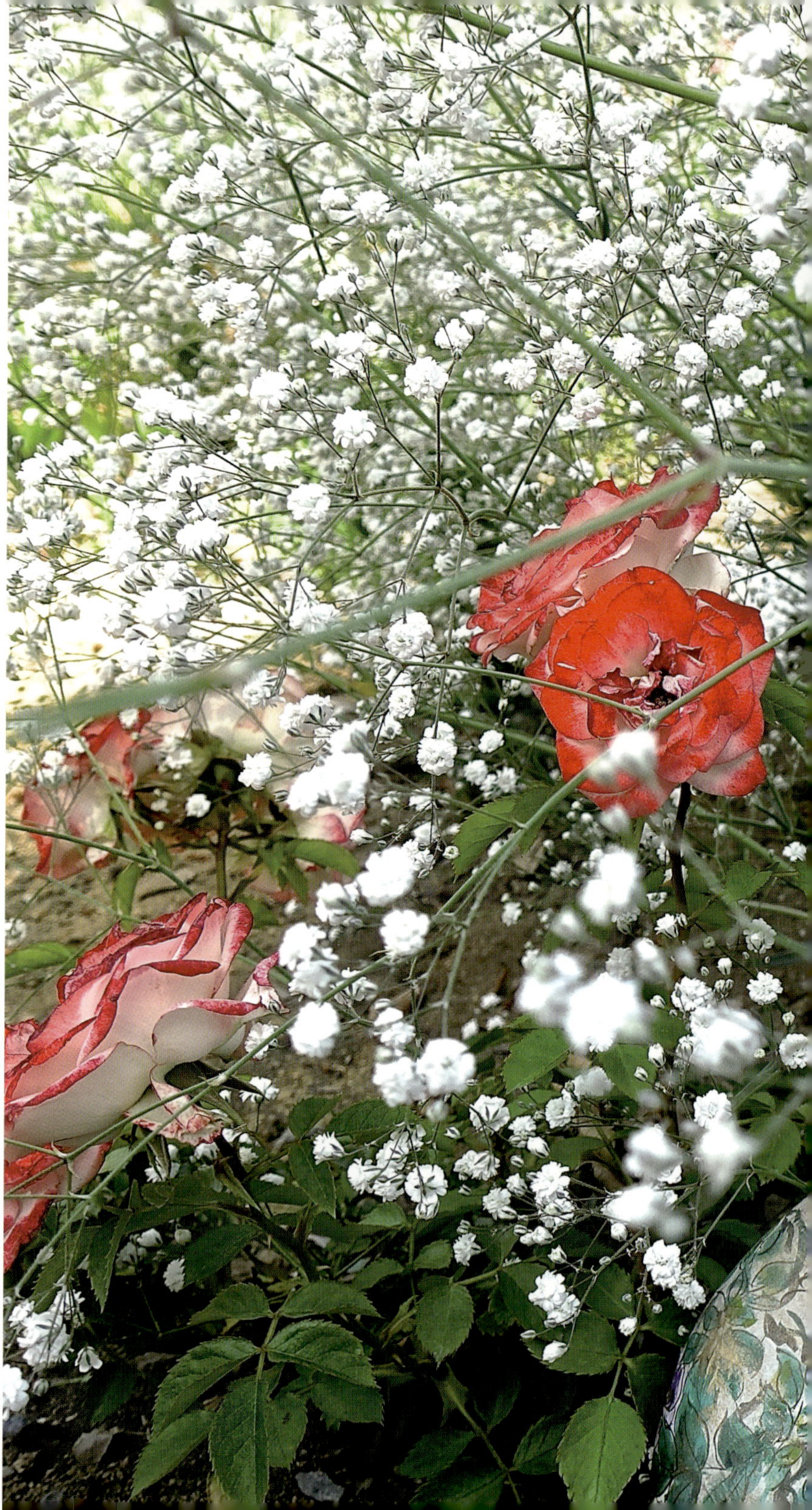

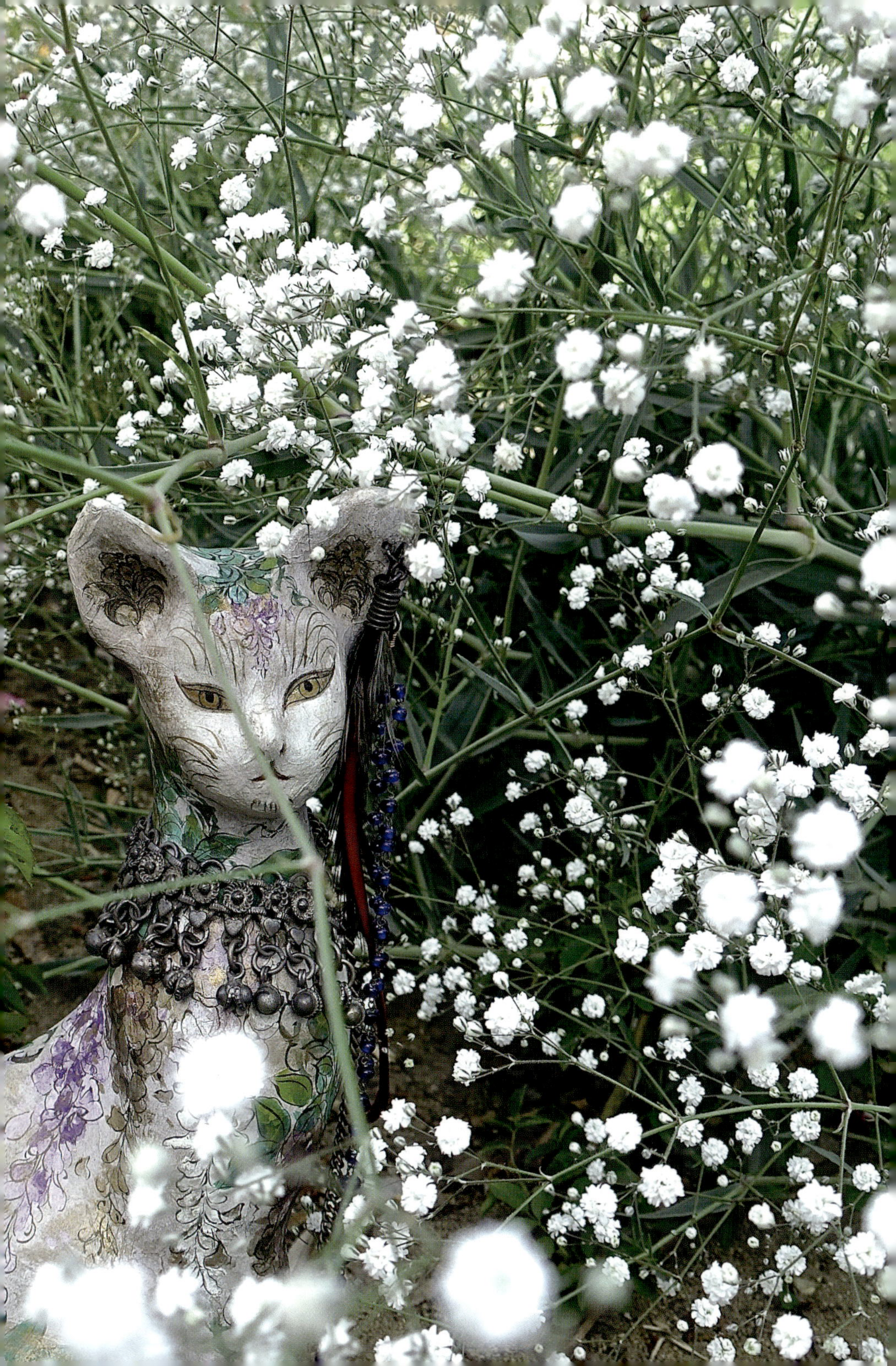

第二部 Part II

第三十四帖　若菜・上 (わかな・じょう)

小松原　末の齢に引かれてや　野辺の若菜も　年をつむべき　　　玉鬘

　（幼い子供たちを連れて、育ての親のあなたの幾久しきご繁栄をお祝いに参りました）

よそに見て折らぬなげきはしげれどもなごり恋しき花の夕かげ　　柏木

　（よそながら垣間見たまま逢えぬ嘆きに、いつまでも恋しさが増さります）

　源氏四十歳の新年、玉鬘が祝賀に若菜を差し上げました。
　その年の春、源氏は出家する朱雀院の希望で末娘の女三の宮と結婚しました。
　何もかも幼い宮に、源氏は紫の上の素晴らしさが今更のように良くわかりましたが、紫の上の心は次第に壊れてゆきます。
　女三の宮は、六条院での蹴鞠を見ていた時に愛猫が御簾から出て、柏木に姿を垣間見られました。そのことで彼女を慕っていた柏木は、宮への想いが更に募ってゆきます。

Chapter 34　Wakana: Jō (Young Herbs I)

[Tamakazura] Komatsubara / Sue no yowai ni / Hikarete ya / Nobe no wakana mo / Toshi o tsumubeki
(With my little children, I come here for Near Year call wishing your prosperity and longevity like young pines as well as young herbs in the field drawn by them.)

[Kashiwagi] Yosoni mite / Oranu nageki wa / Shigeredomo / Nagori koishiki / Hana no Yūkage
(It is so distressing that I cannot pick up the flower I saw across the fence, and my love for that flower I saw on an evening lasts for good.)

On the New Year when Genji becomes 40 years of age, Tamakazura gave him young herbs for celebration.
In the spring of the same year, Genji married Princess Onna-san-no-miya, the unmarried third daughter of the Retired Emperor Suzakuin who is going to become a priest. As the princess is childish in every aspect, Genji realised how excellent Lady Murasaki-no-ue, but her heart begins to break gradually.
When Lady Onna-san-no-miya watched a football game in the Rokujoin Palace, her cat slipped away through the bottom of a bamboo blind and, following the cat, she happened to be seen by Kashiwagi. This caused Kashiwagi, who loved her since before, to deepen the feeling towards her deeper than ever.

79

第三十五帖　若菜・下（わかな・げ）

恋ひわぶる　人の形見と　手馴らせば　なれよ何とて　なく音なるらん　　柏木
　（恋しいあの方の形見と思って可愛がっているのに、どうしてお前は鳴くのだろう）

　女三の宮を忘れられない柏木は、彼女の黒猫をどうにかして引取り、彼女の代わりに可愛がります。そんな時紫の上が大病になり、紫の上につききりな源氏を見て、ますます女三の宮に想いが深まる柏木は、ついに彼女のもとへ忍び込み想いを遂げ、女三の宮は懐妊。そして源氏にもそのことがわかってしまいました。

Chapter 35 Wakana: Ge (Young Herbs II)

[Kashiwagi] Kohi waburu / Hito no katami to Tenarase ba/ Nare yo nani tote / Naku ne naru ran
(I treat you with affection but why do you meow in this way?)

Unable to forget Onna-san-no-miya, Kashiwagi takes in her black cat by overcoming hardships, and cherishes it in place of her.
Lady Murasaki-no-ue has a serious illness so Genji stayed with her the whole time. Looking at this, Kashiwagi feels his longing after Lady Onna-san-no-miya deepens further.
Finally, Kashiwagi steals in her room and fulfilled his wishes. As a result, Lady Onna-san-no-miya gets pregnant.
This is later noticed by Genji.

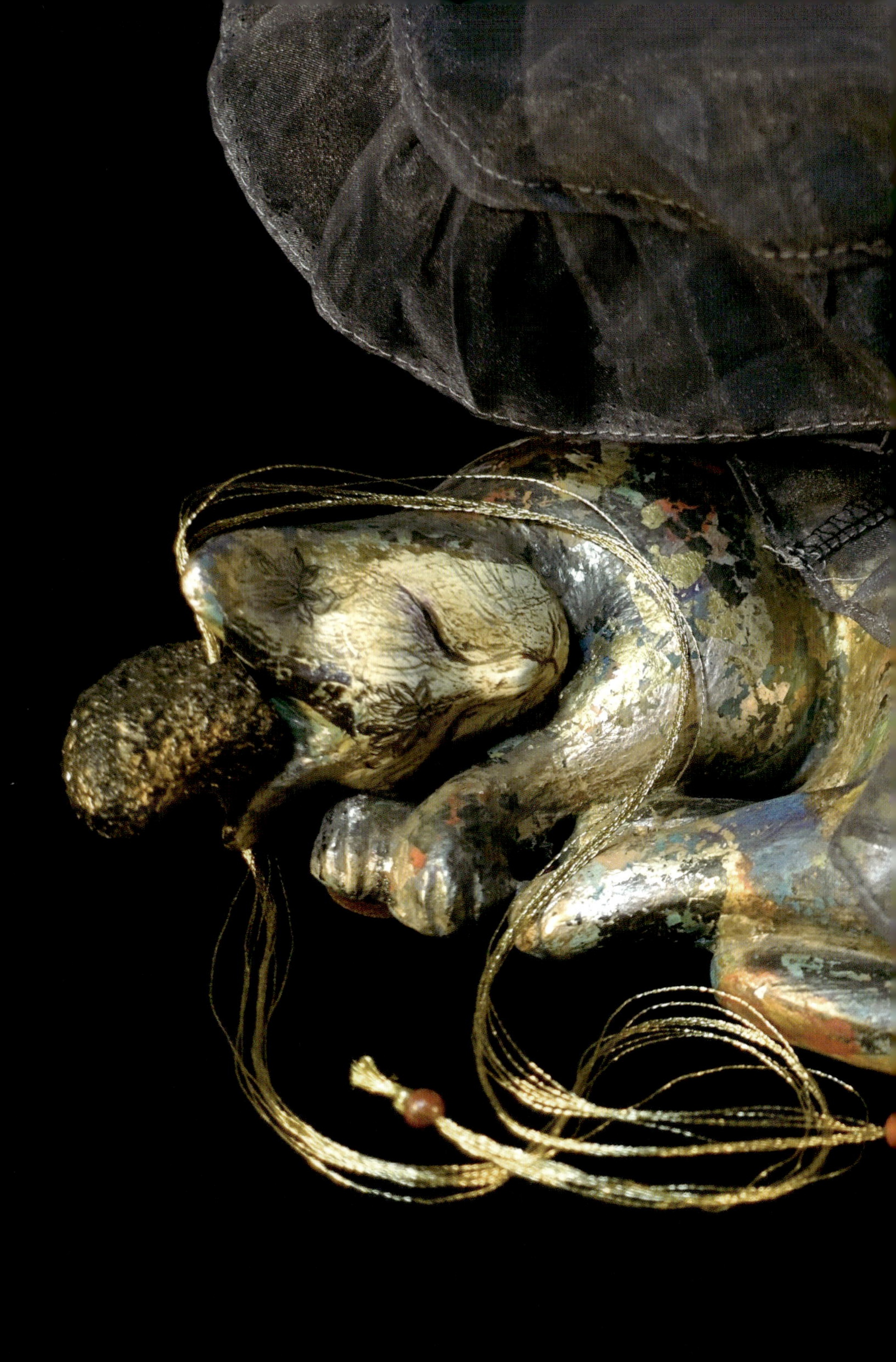

第三十六帖　柏木 (かしはぎ)

行く方なき　空の煙と　なりぬとも
思ふあたりを　立ちは離れじ　　柏木

（当てどのない空の煙となっても、恋しいあなたのおそばを離れはしません）

女三の宮との恋が源氏にわかってしまった柏木は、心労で重い病に掛かり、寝込んでしまいました。
女三の宮は男子 (薫) を出産後、冷たい源氏に悲嘆し、出家してしまいます。
それを知った柏木は重体に陥り、ついに亡くなります。

Chapter 36　Kashiwagi (Oak Tree)

[Kashiwagi] Yukue naki / Sora no keburi to / narinu tomo / Omou Atari o / Tachi wa hanareji
(Even if I became smoke drifting in the sky, I would never leave you, my love.)

Knowing that the affair with Lady Onna-san-no-miya is known by Genji, Kashiwagi fell ill by worries and becomes unable to leave his bed.
Lady Onna-san-no-miya gives birth to a boy (Kaoru) but, heartbroken by the cold attitude of Genji, she enters a nunnery.
Hearing the news, Kashiwagi took a critical turn and eventually deceased.

第三十七帖　横笛（よこぶえ）

横笛の　調べはことに　変わららぬ　むなしくなりし　音こそつきせね　　　夕霧

（横笛の音は変わっていませんので、故人の奏でた音色はいつまでも伝えられることでしょう）

　柏木の親友・夕霧は、柏木の遺言どおり、未亡人になった落葉の宮をたびたびお見舞いします。宮の母・一条御息所から御礼に柏木の横笛を送られると、その夜夢に柏木が現れ、笛を伝えたい人は他にあることを告げました。夕霧は源氏にその旨を相談すると、源氏は「わけあって、その笛を預かろう」と申し出ました。

Chapter 37　Yokobue (Flute)

[Yūgiri] Yokobue no / Shirabe wa kotoni / Kawaranu o / Munashiku narishi / Ne koso tsukisene
(The tone played by the departed will be handed down forever because the sound of flute does not change.)

Yūgiri, the best friend of Kashiwagi frequently inquires after Lady Ochiba-no-miya who is his window, by following the wishes left by the departed friend.
On the night after he received the flute of Kashiwagi as a return present from the mother of Lady Ochiba-no-miya, Kashiwagi appeared in his dream telling that he has an intention to present the flute to a person other than Yūgiri...
Yūgiri consulted Genji about the dream; Genji proposed to him that Genji keep the flute in custody.

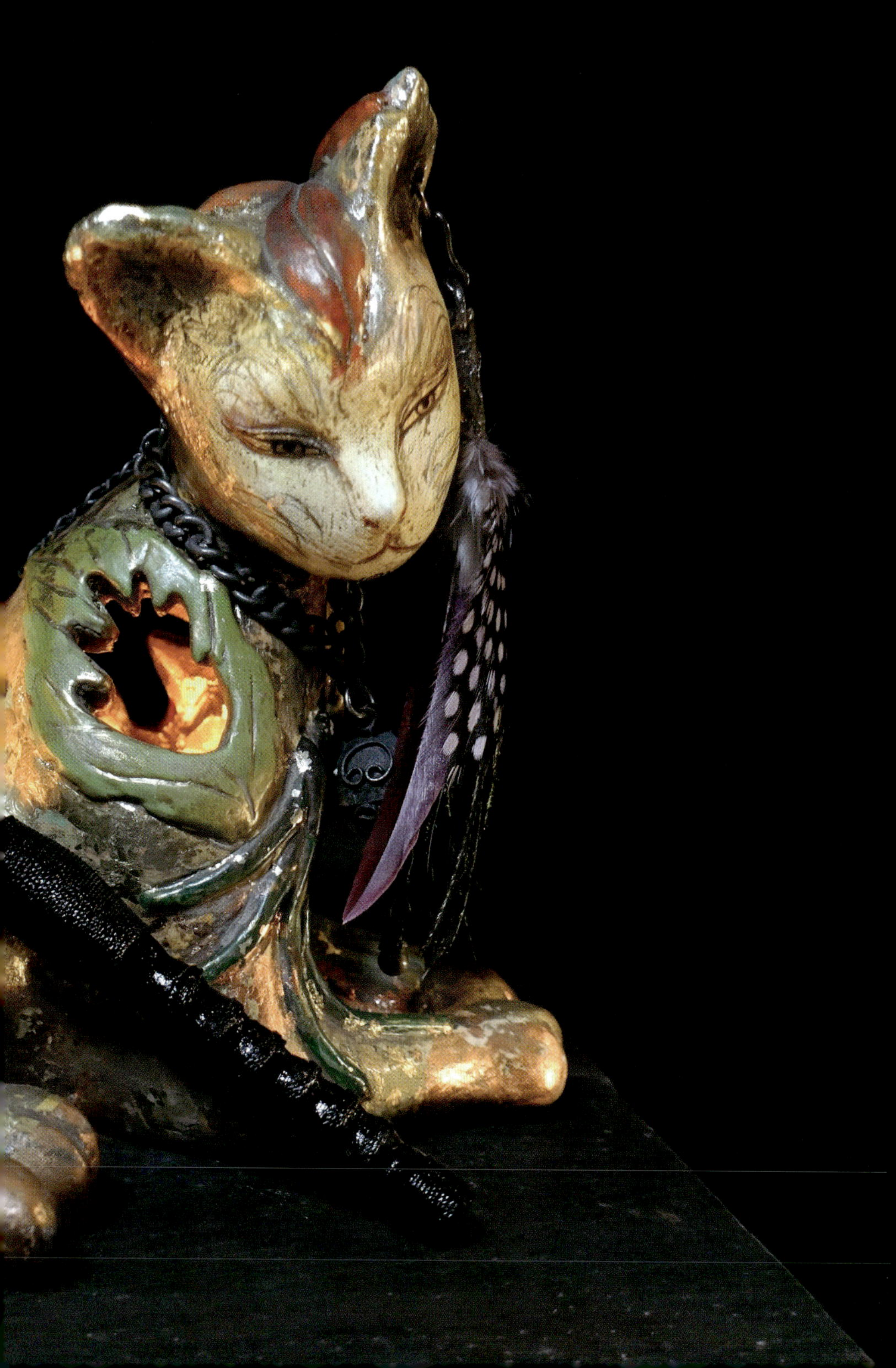

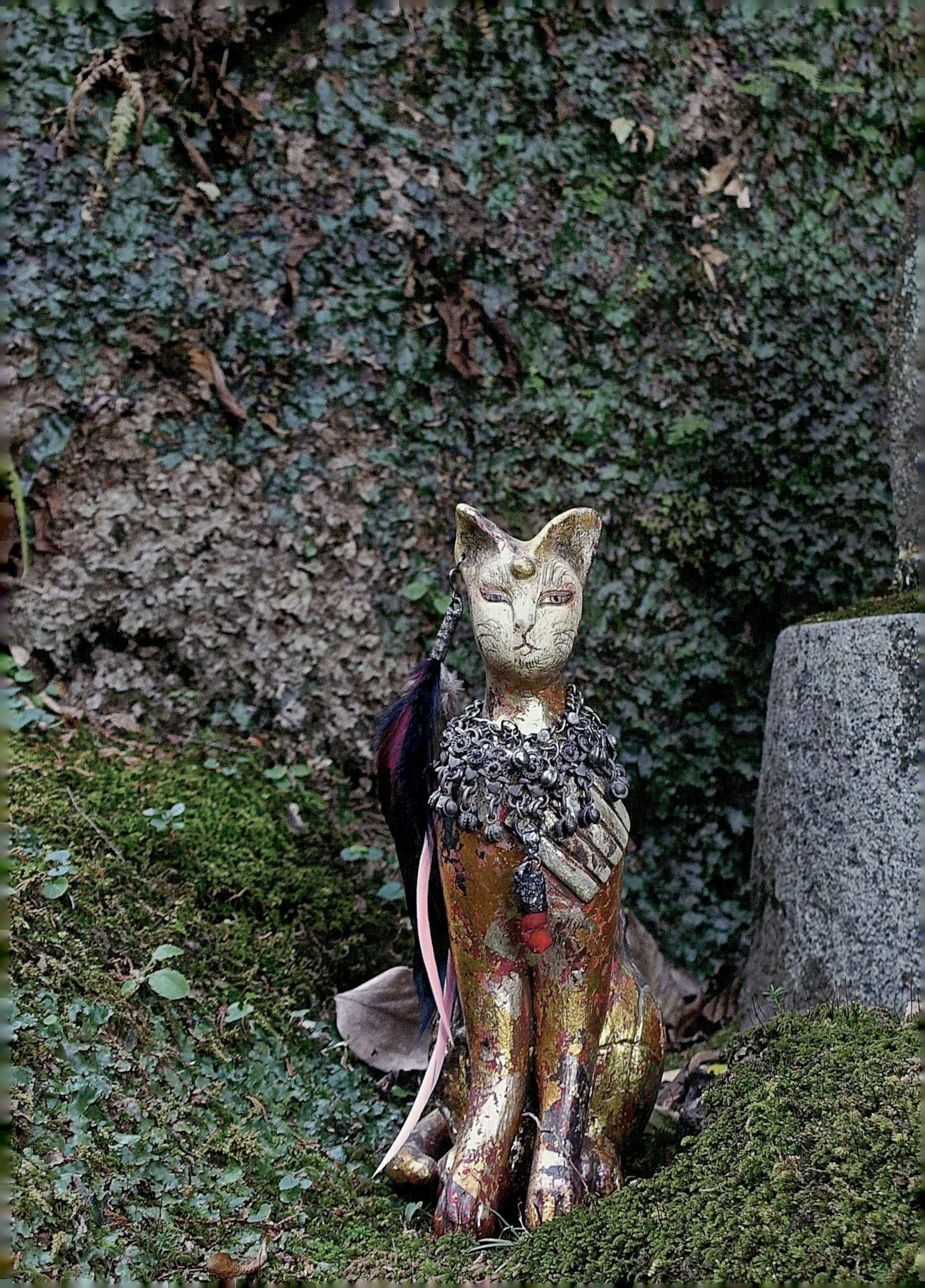

第三十八帖 鈴虫 (すずむし)

大方の 秋をば憂しと 知りにしを
ふり棄てがたし 鈴虫の声　女三の宮

(秋といえば辛いものと思い知りましたが、鈴虫の声を聞くと、その秋も振り棄てにくいものです)

雲の上を かけはなれたる 住みかにも
もの忘れせぬ 秋の夜の月　冷泉院

(帝位を去った自分の住処にも、忘れず秋の名月は照っている)

源氏が出家した女三の宮の部屋で、鈴虫の音を愛でながら琴を弾いていると、蛍兵部卿の宮や夕霧が訪れました。管弦の宴に盛り上がったところに冷泉院からお召があり、一同は院のもとへ集い、詩歌管弦の宴になりました。冷泉院は、帝時代には出来なかった実父・源氏との気軽な対面を喜ぶのでした。

Chapter 38 **Suzumushi** (Bell Cricket)

Onna-san-no-miya/ Okata no / Aki o ba ushi to /Shiri nishi o / Furisute gataki / Suzumushi no koe

(Though I know that the autumn is mostly a bitter season, the songs of bell crickets make me realise that I should not give up on the autumn so easily.)

[Retired Emperor Reizei] Kumo no ue o / Kakehanaretaru / Sumika nimo / Monowasure senu / Aki no yo no tsuki

(Even after having retired from the post of Emperor, the autumn moon does not forget to illuminate my palace.)

When Genji is playing the koto in the room of Lady Onna-san-no-miya who left it for entering a nunnery, Bridge Hotaru Hyobukyo-no-Miya and Yugiri visit him, so they start a concert party. About the time the party grows livelier, the Retired Emperor Reizei invited them so they went to his palace and continued the party with poems and music. The Retired Emperor Reizei was very glad to meet Genji, his biological father, casually for this was impossible when he was the emperor.

第三十九帖　夕霧(ゆふぎり)

山里の　あはれを添ふる　夕霧に
たち出でん空も　なき心地して　　夕霧

　（山里の淋しさを増す夕霧が立ちこめて、どちらの空に
　立ち出でてよいものか、去ることも出来ない心地です）

　夕霧は柏木の未亡人・落葉の宮を見舞いに訪れるうちに、宮への恋心が募ってゆきました。宮の母・一条御息所はそれを心配しながら書いた手紙が、夕霧の妻・雲居の雁に奪われ、返事が来ないので落胆して亡くなります。夕霧は、母の死により一層彼を拒む落葉の宮と、どうにかして結婚するのでした。

Chapter 39 Yūgiri (Evening Mist)

[Yūgiri] Yamazato no / Aware o souru / Yūgiri ni / Tachiiden sora mo /Naki kokochi site
(In the evening mist deepening the pathetic mood of this mountain village, I do not know in which direction to set off.)

Visiting the Lady Ochiba-no-miya frequently after the death of her husband Kashiwagi, Yūgiri's love for her deepens more and more.
Mother of the widow, Ichijo-no-miyasudokoro gets anxious about Yūgiri's state and wrote a letter to him, but the letter is hidden by Kumoi-no-kari who is the Yūgiri's wife. Because Ichijo-no-miyasudokoro cannot receive the reply from Yūgiri, she was disappointed to death.
The death of the mother of Lady Ochiba-no-miya increased the resistance, but Yūgiri managed to marry her eventually.

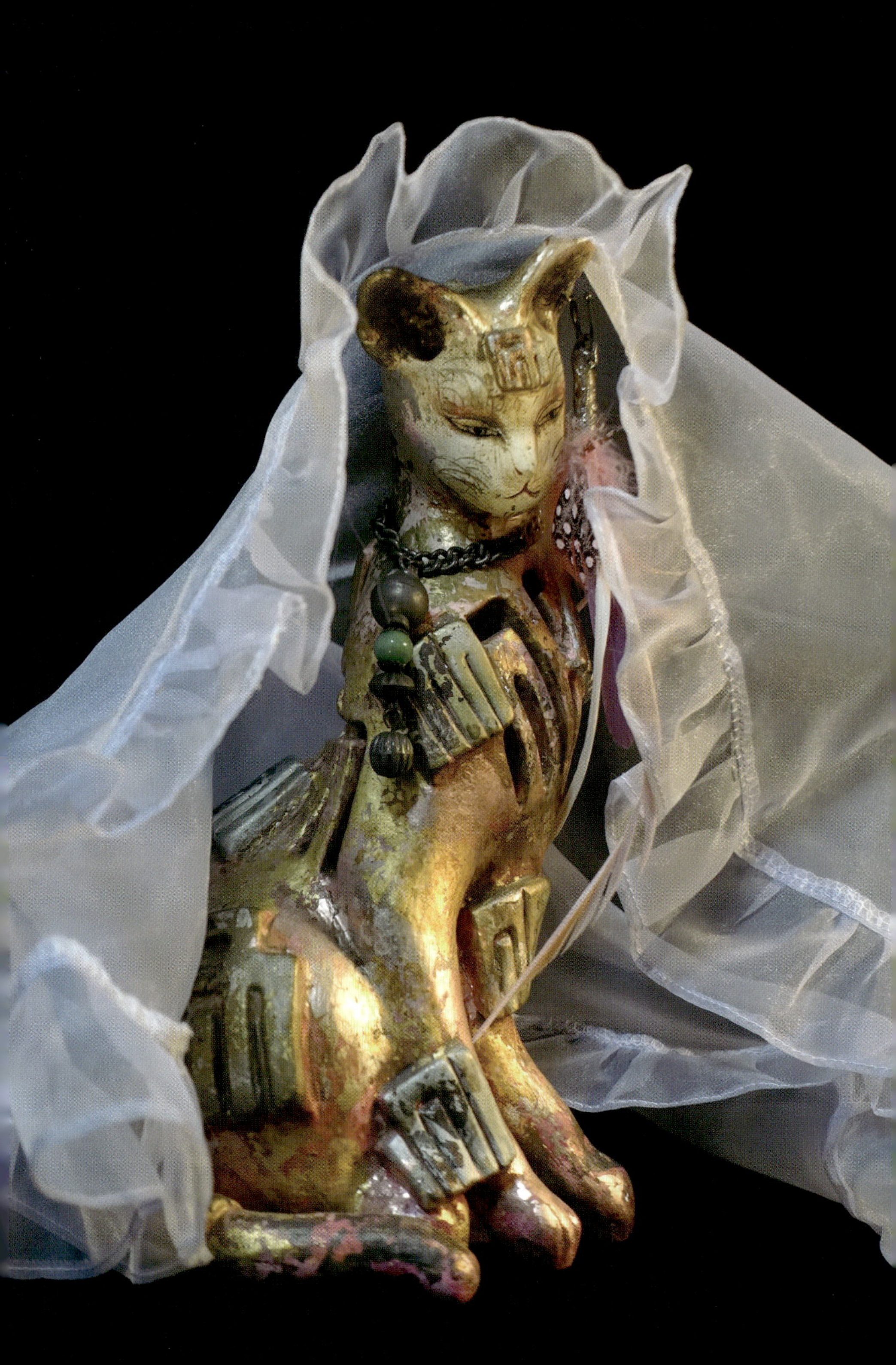

第四十帖　御法(みのり)

絶えぬべき　御法ながらぞ　頼まるる
世々にと結ぶ　中の契りを　　　紫の上

（これが最後の法会ですが、御法をご縁にあなたとはまたあの世でお目に掛かれると存じます）

　大病後の紫の上は、体調が思わしくなく、出家願望も源氏に許されません。
　紫の上発願の法華経供養が行われた時は、帝や夕霧、東宮、后の宮たちをはじめ、多くの人が志を寄せた盛大な催になりました。
　そして大勢の人々から愛された紫の上は、最後に源氏と明石の中宮に看取られて、露の消え入るように静かに亡くなります。

Chapter 40　Minori (The Law)

[Murasaki-no-ue] Taenubeki / Minori nagara zo / Tanomaruru / Yoyo ni to musubu / Naka no chigiri o
(This is the last religious service, but the eternal Buddhist law will allow me to meet you by the tie that binds us throughout the past, present and future.)

Since the serious ill, Lady Murasaki-no-ue is in a poor health condition, but her wish to become a nun is not permitted by Genji.
A Buddhist rite is held by the request from Lady Murasaki-no-ue. It becomes a magnificent event thanks to the gifts and offerings from many people including the Emperor, Yūgiri, Crown Prince and his ladies.
Finally, Lady Murasaki-no-ue who is loved by many persons passed away quietly like the mist disappears with attendance of Genji and Empress Akashi on her deathbed.

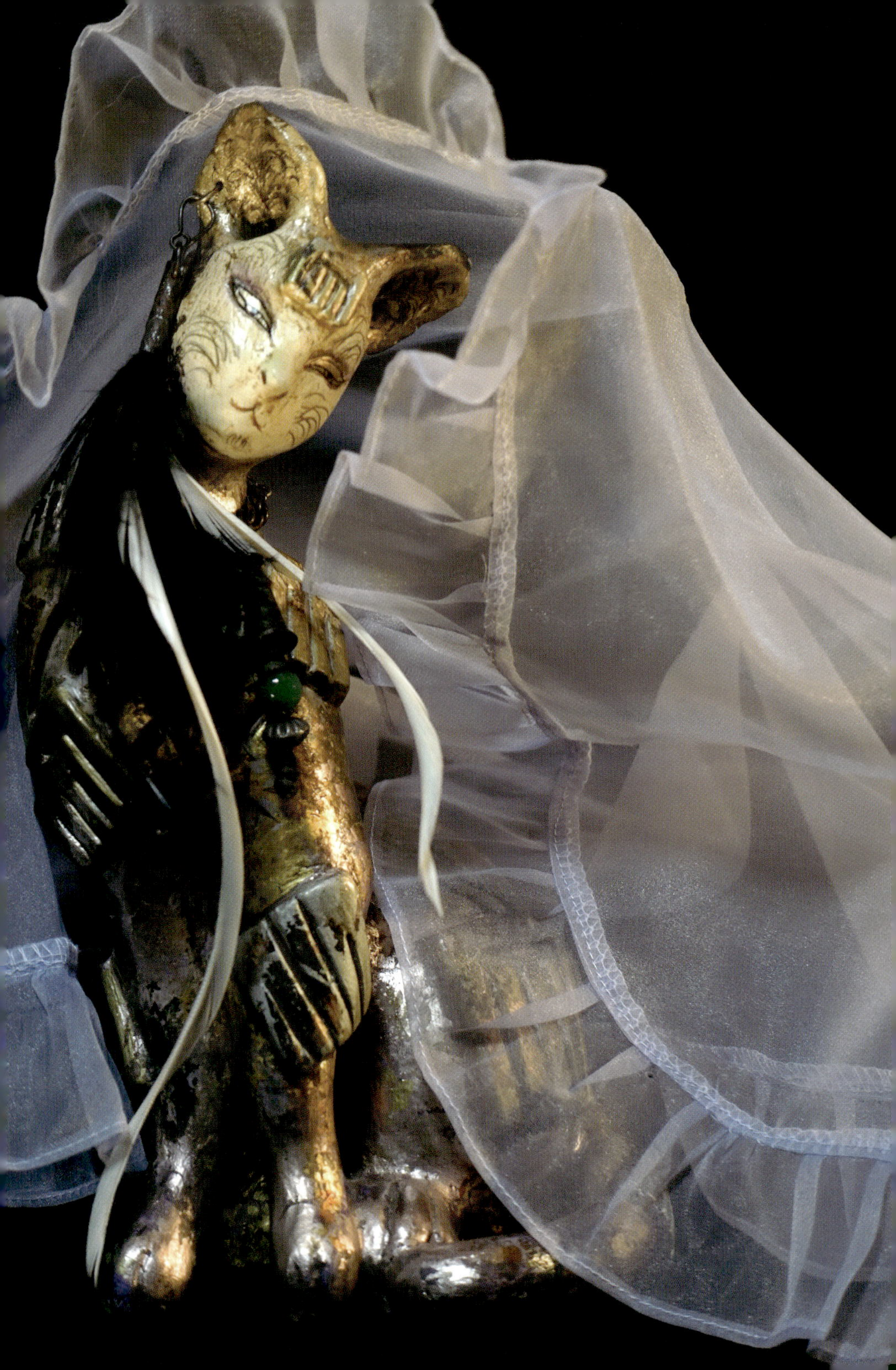

第四十一帖　幻（まぼろし）

大空を　かよふまぼろし　夢にだに
見えこぬ魂の　行く方たづねよ　　源氏

　（大空を行き通う幻術士よ、夢にも現れぬあの人の魂の行方を探し出しておくれ）

　紫の上を失った源氏は、春につけ、夏につけ、花を見ても蛍を見ても、共に過ごした季節の行事など来るたびに涙にくれ、その悲哀はいっこうに癒えません。
　そして以前からの念願の出家を決意し、その準備を始めました。

Chapter 41　Maboroshi (Wizard)

[Genji] Ōzora o / Kayou maboroshi / Yume ni da ni / Miekonu tama no / Yukue tazuneyo
(Oh. wizard travelling the skies, find the spirit that does not appear even in my dreams.)

After losing Murasaki-no-ue, Genji cannot stand shedding tears in any event that reminds him of her, in the spring, in the summer, upon viewing flowers or viewing fireflies. His grief seems never to be cured.
Finally, Genji decided to realise his old wish of becoming a priest and he begins preparation for renouncing the world.

◉雲隠（くもかくれ）
※タイルは源氏香を模した作品

◉Kumogakure (Gone into the Clouds)
*Tiles representing the Genji-kō incenses

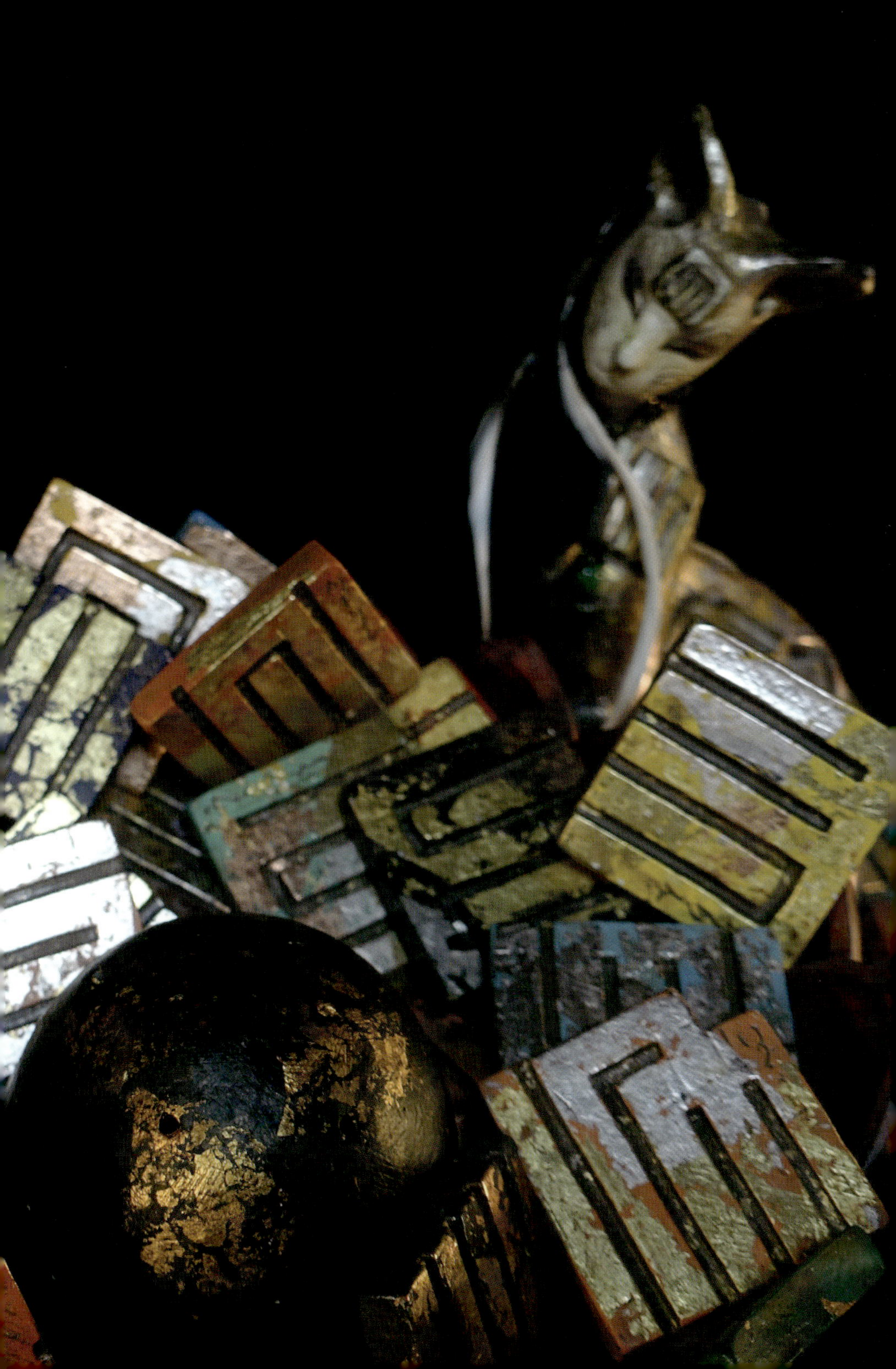

第三部　宇治十帖
Part III　Uji Chapters

第四十二帖　匂宮 (にほふのみや)

かくあやしきまで人の咎むる香にしみたまへるを、兵部卿宮なん他事よりいどましく思して、それは、わざとよろづのすぐれたるうつしをしめたまひ…

（こうして中将には不思議なまでに人のあやしむ香りが染みついていらっしゃるのを、兵部卿宮は、ほかの何よりも負けたくないとお思いになられて、特にあらゆる香をお焚き染めになり…）

　時は移り、今は源氏を偲ばせる貴人は今上天皇の三の宮・匂宮と女三の宮の若君・薫です。
　薫には生まれつき芳香があり、匂宮はそれに張り合って薫物に心を砕いているので「匂う兵部卿、薫中将」と世間にもてはやされるようになります。

Chapter 42　Niō-no-Miya (Perfumed Prince)

Kaku ayashiki made hito no togamuru kō ni shimitamaeru o, Hyobukyo-no-miya nam tagoto yori idomashiku omoite, sore wa waza to yorozu no suguretaru utsushi o shimetamai….
(The General has a fragrance that mysteriously stimulates the senses of people. This generated competitive energy of the Prince, who does not want to be inferior in any way to others and tried all kinds of excellent incenses…)

Now that the time has passed, the only noblemen who remind the presence of Genji were Prince Niō-no-miya, the third son of the current Emperor and Kaoru, the son of Lady Onna-san-no-miya...
Kaoru has a fragrance by birth and Prince Niō-no-miya is especially attentive to incense as if he tries to compete with him. Now people make a fuss over them, calling them "The Perfumed Highness and the Fragrant General".

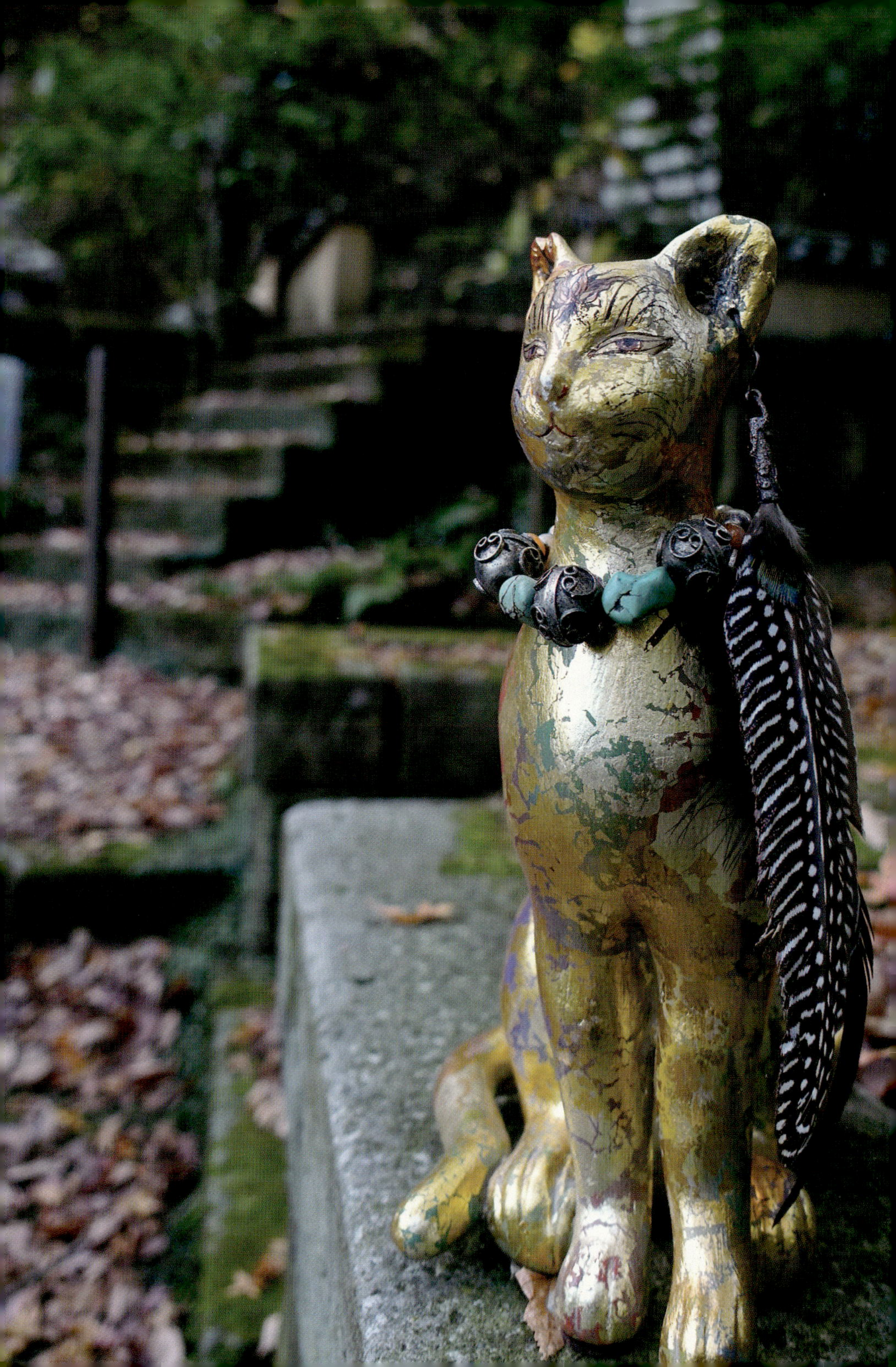

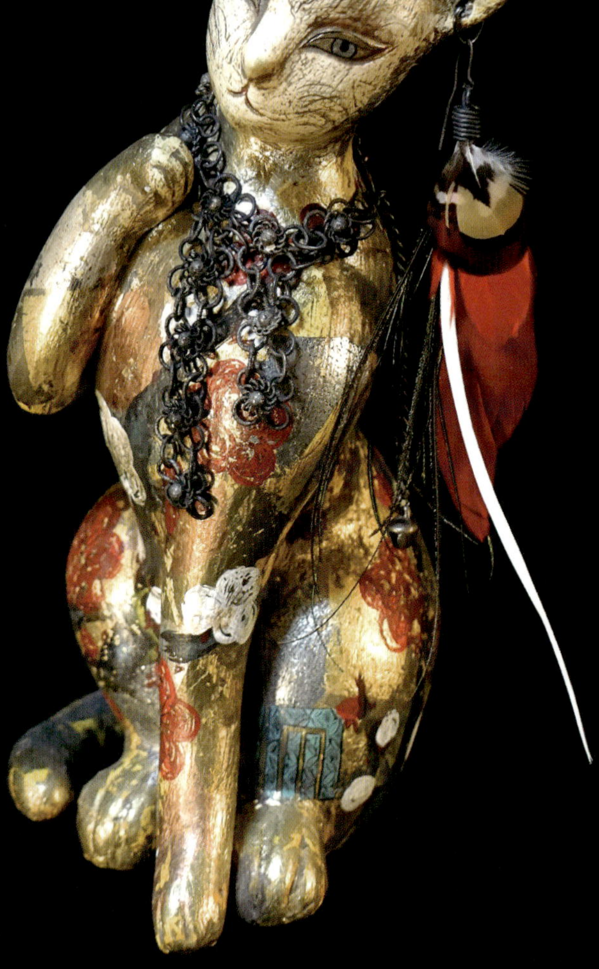

第四十三帖　紅梅(こうばい)

心ありて　風の匂わす　園の梅に　まづ鴬の　訪はずやあるべき　　　按察使大納言

　　（心があって、風が匂いを送る園の梅に、何はさておき鴬の訪れぬはずがありましょうか）

花の香に　誘はれぬべき　身なりせば　風のたよりを　過ぐさましやは　　　匂宮

　　（花の香にすぐ誘われるような私ならば、風の便りをただ聞き過ごしましょうか）

　　按察使大納言は前妻との娘が二人、妻の連れ子・宮の御方と姫君が三人いました。
　　大納言は姉を東宮妃として入内させ、妹は東宮の弟・匂宮との結婚を希望し、宮に紅梅を添えて歌を贈りますが、匂宮は宮の御方に惹かれていました。

Chapter 43　Kōbai (Red Plum)

[Azechi Dainagon] Kokoro arite / Kaze no niowasu / Sono no ume ni / Mazu uguisu no / Towazu ya arubeki
(How could the bush warblers not visit the garden plums that have minds and transmit smell on the wind?)

[Prince Niō-no-miya] Hana no ka ni / Sasowarenubeki / Mi nariseba / Kaze no tayori o / Sugusamasshi ya wa
(I am a kind of man who is immediately tempted by the scent of flowers so how could I let pass the message borne on the wind?)

Azechi Dainagon has three daughters, including two borne between him and the previous wife and Miya-no-okata who is the child by a former marriage of the current wife.
He plans to let the elder sister enter the Imperial Court as the wife of the Crown Prince and the younger sister marry to Prince Niō-no-miya, younger brother of the Crown Prince. He sends a message poem asking marriage to Prince Niō-no-miya together with red plum blossoms, but the prince is charmed more by Miya-no-okata.

第四十四帖　竹河(たけかわ)

竹河の　橋のつめなるや　橋のつめなるや
花園に　我をば放てや　少女めざしたぐへて（催馬楽・竹河）

（竹川の橋のたもとにある斎宮の花園に、私を遊ばせて下さい、貴女を伴って）

　玉鬘は髯黒大将との間に男子三人と女子二人あり、美しい姫君たちは求婚者が沢山いて、玉鬘を悩ませていました。薫は玉鬘を姉のように慕い、玉鬘邸でも評判の良い貴公子です。
　三月、桜の花盛りの頃、姫君たちは庭の桜を掛けて碁を打ちました。

Chapter 44　Takekawa (Bamboo River)

[Takeuchi, ancient vocal court music] Takekawa no / Hashi no tsume naru ya /Hashi no tsume naru ya / Hanazono ni hare / Hanazono ni / Ware o ba hanate ya / Ware o ba hanate ya / Mezashi taguete
(Please let me play in the flower garden by the bridge of the Bamboo River, together with you.)

Tamakazura has three sons and two daughters between General Higekuro. The beautiful daughters attracted many suitors, which caused worries of Tamakazura. Kaoru adores Tamakazura as if she is his sister, and has also a good reputation in the mansion of Tamakazura.
In March when the cherry blossoms are in full bloom, the daughters played the game of go by betting cherty flowers in the garden.

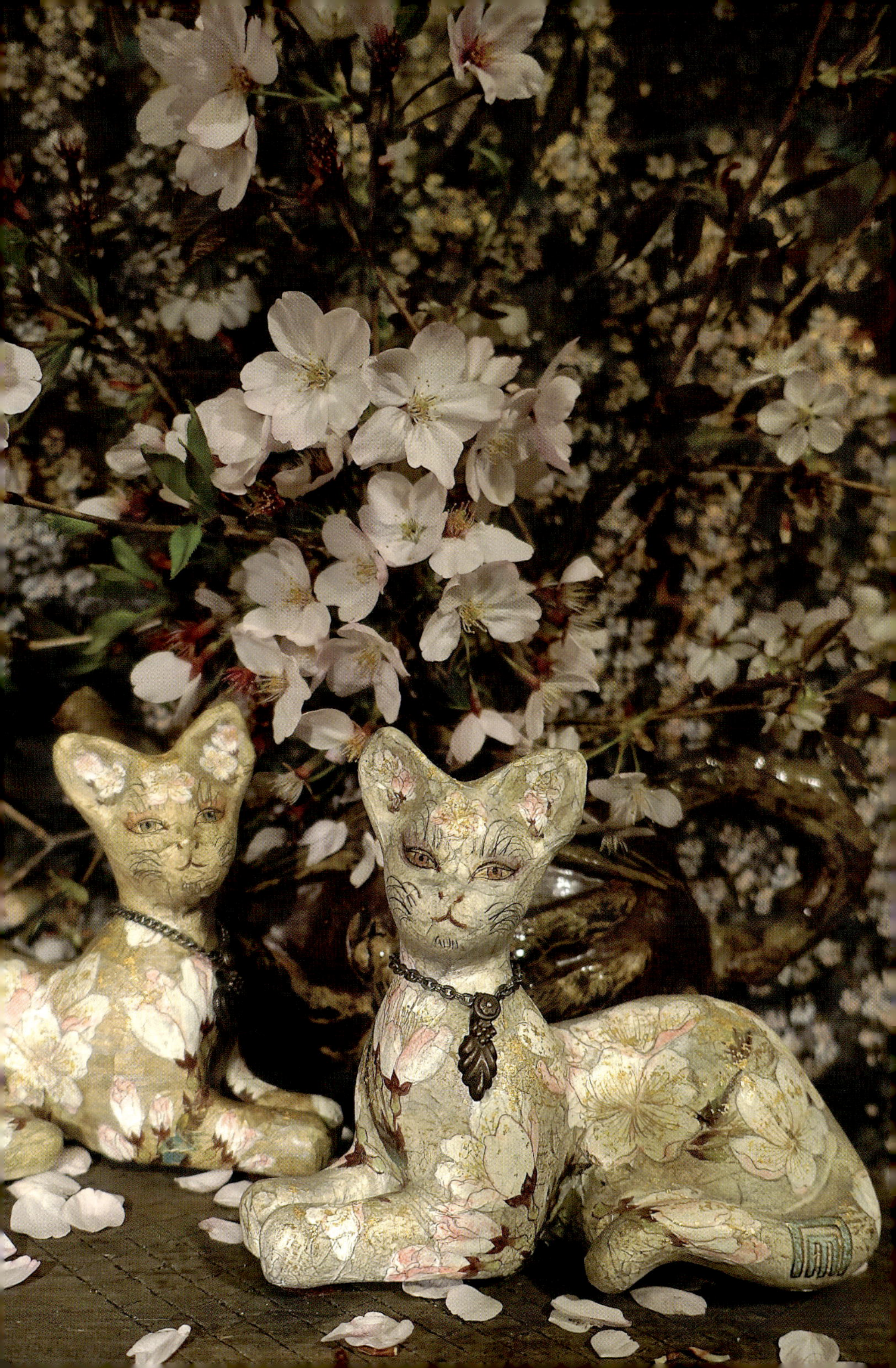

第四十五帖　橋姫 (はしひめ)

橋姫の　心を汲みて　高瀬さす　棹のしづくに　袖ぞ濡れぬる　　薫

　　(姫君たちのお心をお察しして、棹の滴に袖が濡れるように私も涙で袖が濡れてしまいます)

　　薫は宇治の山荘に隠棲している源氏の弟・八宮のもとへ、仏道を縁に度々訪れるようになります。
　　八宮には、大君と中君という二人の美しい姫君がいました。
　　薫は大君に想いを寄せるようになり、薫から宇治の姫君の話を聞いた匂宮は、宇治への興味を持つのでした。

Chapter 45　Hashihime (Princesses of Bridge)

[Kaoru] Hashihime no / Kokoro o kumite / Takase sasu / Sao no shizuku ni / Sode zo nurenuru
(Considering the minds of the daughters, my sleeves are wet with tears just like the sleeves of the boat rower getting drenched by the drops from the pole.)

Recently, Kaoru often visits Prince Hachinomiya, a younger brother of Genji leading a secluded life in a mountain cottage in Uji, to talk about the Buddhism.
Prince Hachinomiya lives with two beautiful daughters, Ōikimi and Nakanokimi.
Kaoru begins to take a fancy to Ōikimi, and Niō-no-miya who heard about the sisters in Uji from Kaoru takes interest in them.

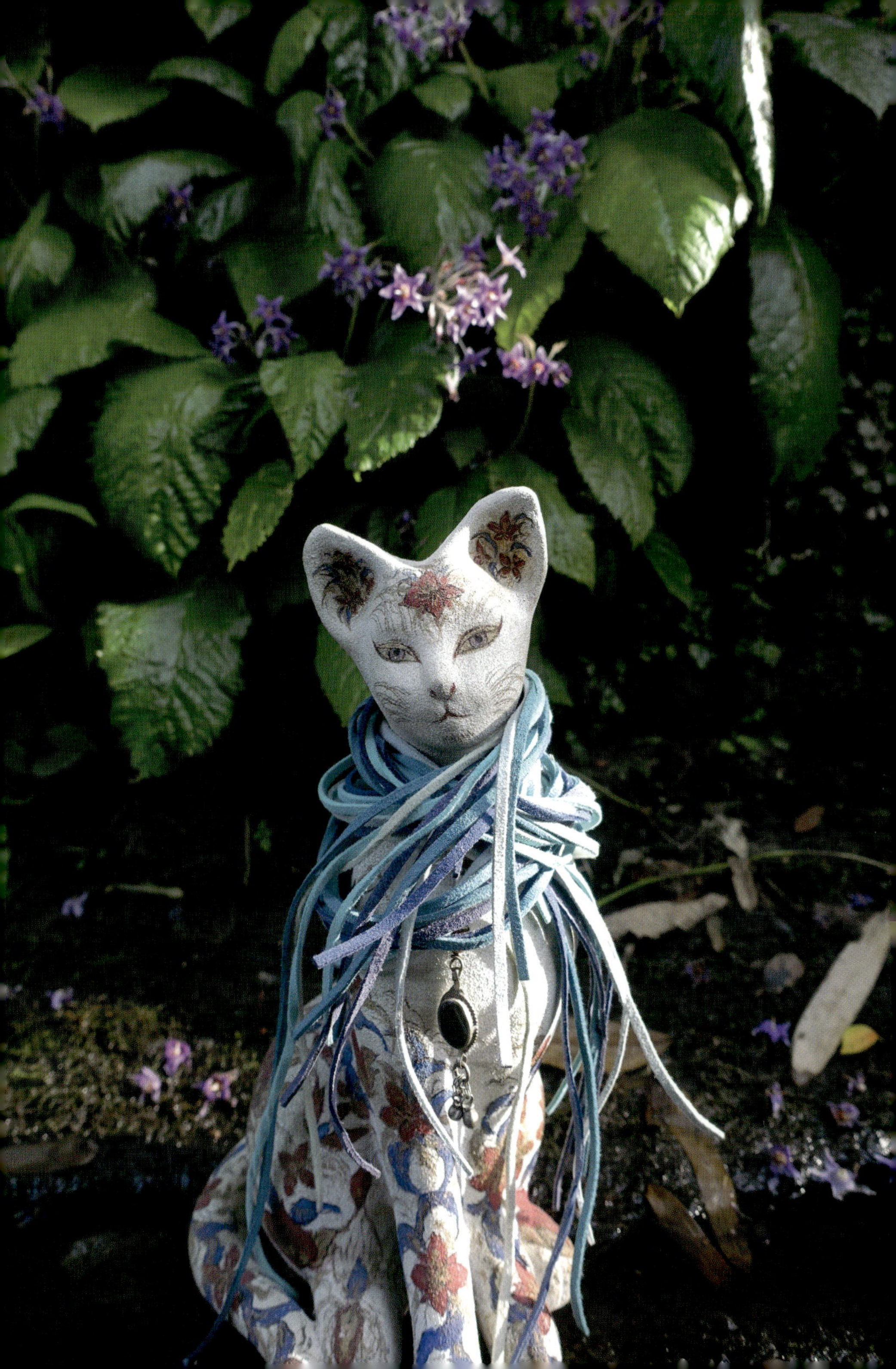

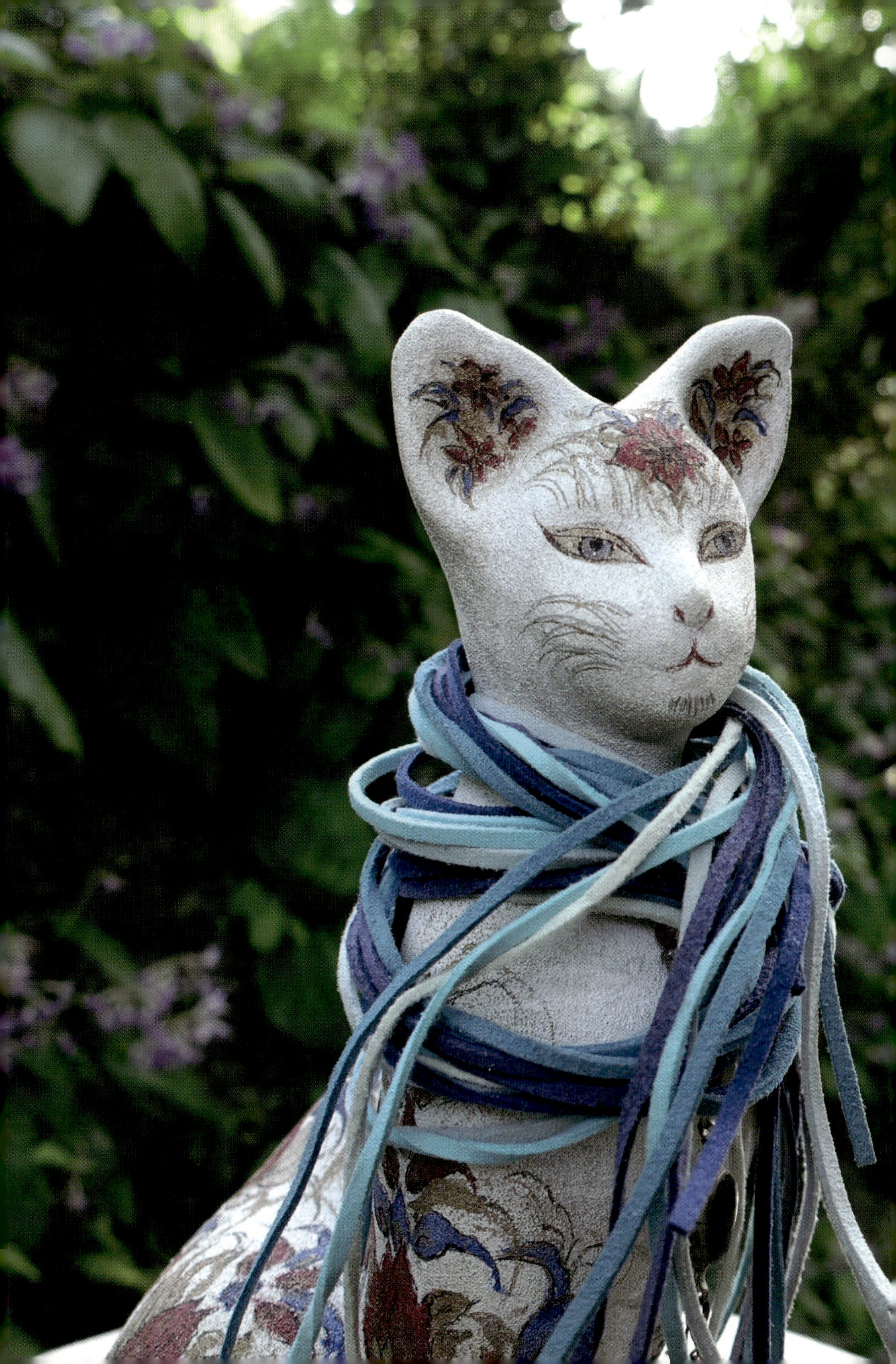

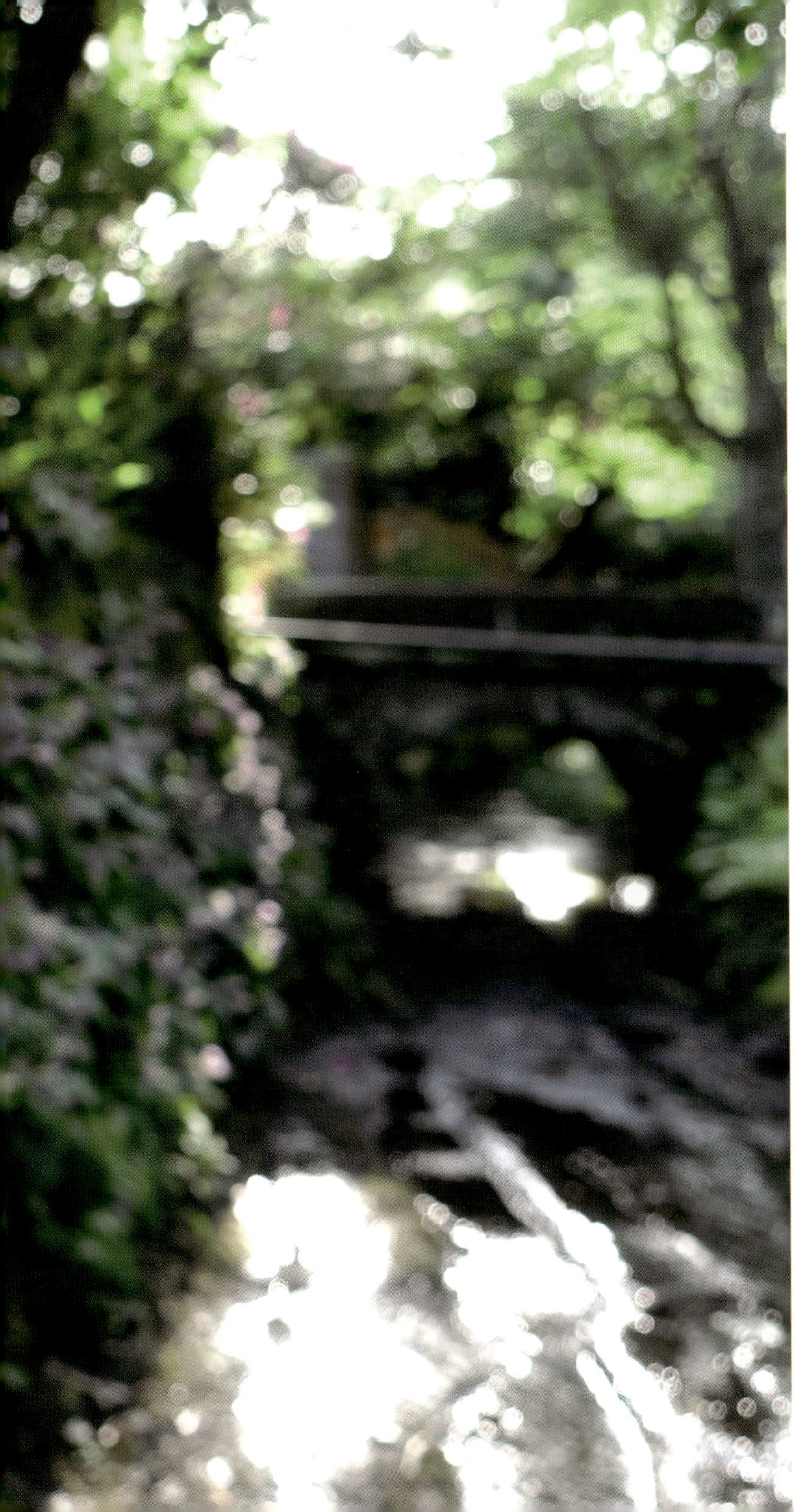

第四十六帖　椎本（しひがもと）

立ち寄らむ　蔭とたのみし　椎が本　むなしき床に　なりにけるかな　　薫

（法の師にもとお頼みしていた宮はすでに亡く、その後仏間もむなしき床になってしまった）

　宇治の八宮が、薫に二人の娘の行く末を託して亡くなります。
　山深い宇治の地に残された姫君たちの哀しさと心細さは、ひとしおでした。薫は八宮を偲ぶとともに、大君に恋心を打ち明け、匂宮は中の君との取持ちを薫にせがみます。

Chapter 46　Shī ga Moto (At the Foot of Lithocarpus Tree)

[Kaoru] Tachiyoran / Kage to tanomishi / Shī ga moto / Munashiki toko ni / Narini keru kana
(The Prince I relied on as my teacher of Buddhist Law is gone and the altar room left behind has become just an empty floor.)

Prince Hachinomiya deceased after entrusting the future of his daughters to Kaoru.
The sorrow and loneliness of the sisters are enhanced much more for they are left in a distant mountainous area of Uji.
Kaoru keeps on thinking of the late Hachinomiya but he also confesses his love to Ōikimi. Meanwhile, Niō-no-miya pesters him to introduce Niō-no-miya to Nakanokimi.

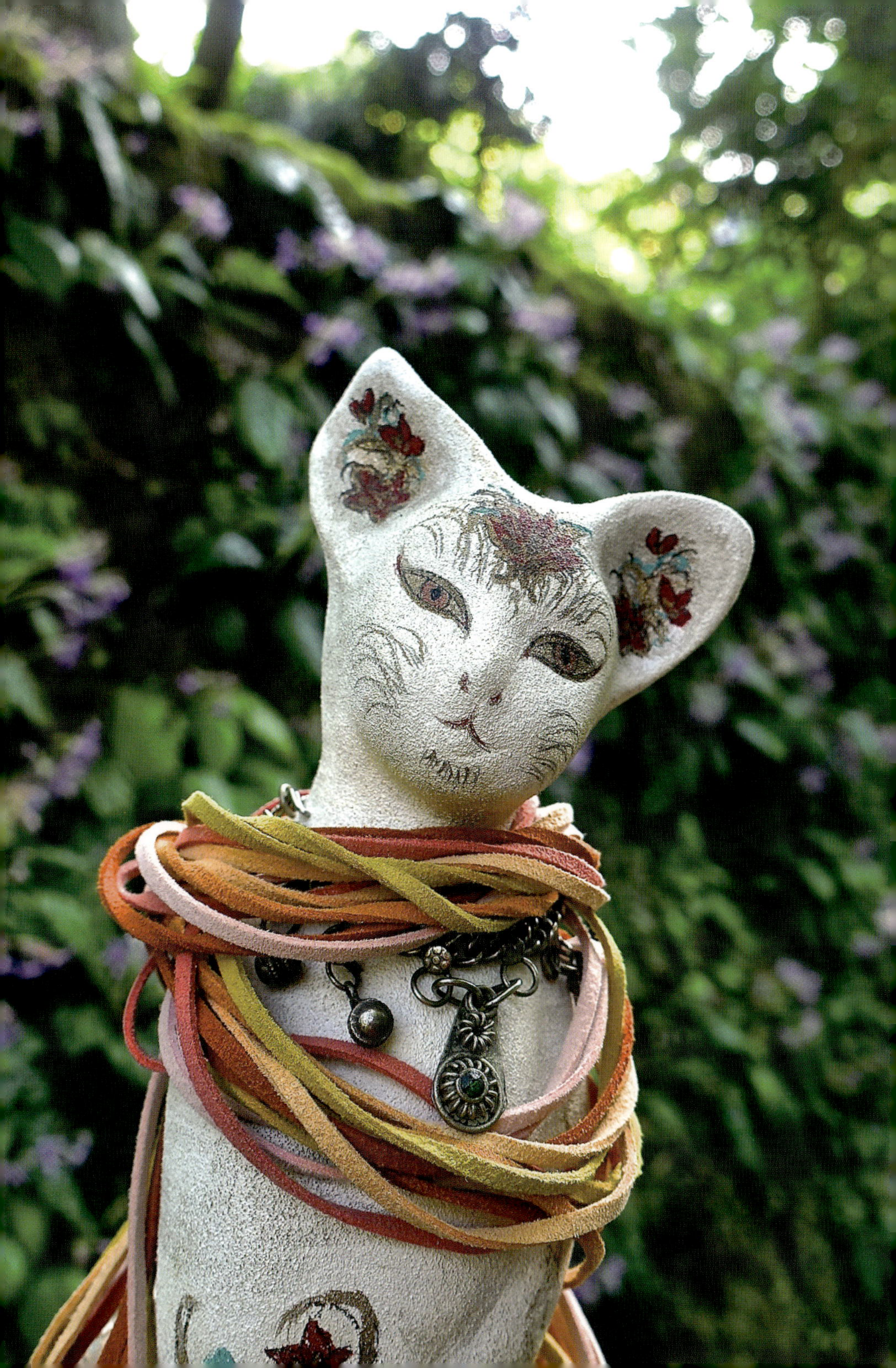

第四十七帖　總角 (あげまき)

あげまきに　長き契りを　むすびこめ
おなじ所に　よりもあはなむ　　　薫

　（あぎまき結びに末長い契りをこめて、ぜひ一緒になりたいものです）

ぬきもあへず　もろき涙の　玉の緒に
長き契りを　いかがむすばん　　　大君

　（繋ぎとめもできずに散る涙の玉のように儚い命なのに、末長い契りなどどうして結べましょう）

　薫は大君に求婚しますが、大君は彼に中の君との結婚を勧めます。そこで、薫は以前から頼まれていた匂宮と中の君との仲を取持ち、大君に恨まれます。
　しかし匂宮は身分柄遠い宇治になかなか訪問できず、都での縁談も進んでいることを知った二人の落胆は大きいものでした。
　そのうち大君は衰弱して亡くなってしまい、薫はとても深く嘆きます。

Chapter 47　Agemaki (Trefoil Knot)

[Kaoru] Agemaki ni / Nagaki Chigiri o / Musubi kome / Onaji tokoro ni / Yorimo awanan
(I wish you and me become together by twining vows into a long-lasting, tight trefoil knot.)

[Ōikimi] Nuki mo aezu / Moroki namida no / Tama no o ni / Nagaki chigiri o / Ikaga musuban
(Life is like fragile teardrops that are scattered without being able to be kept, so how could we exchange vows that lasts forever?)

Kaoru proposed to Ōikimi, but she recommends him to marry Nakanokimi.
Nevertheless, Kaoru mediated the association between Niō-no-miya and Nakanokimi as pestered by him since before, which made Ōikimi blames on Kaoru.
Because of his high position, however, Niō-no-miya cannot find an opportunity to visit Uji easily. In addition, the two sisters were also disappointed considerably knowing that the plan to marry him to another woman is in progress in Kyoto.
Soon, Ōikimi grows feeble and finally deceased. This caused deep sorrow of Kaoru.

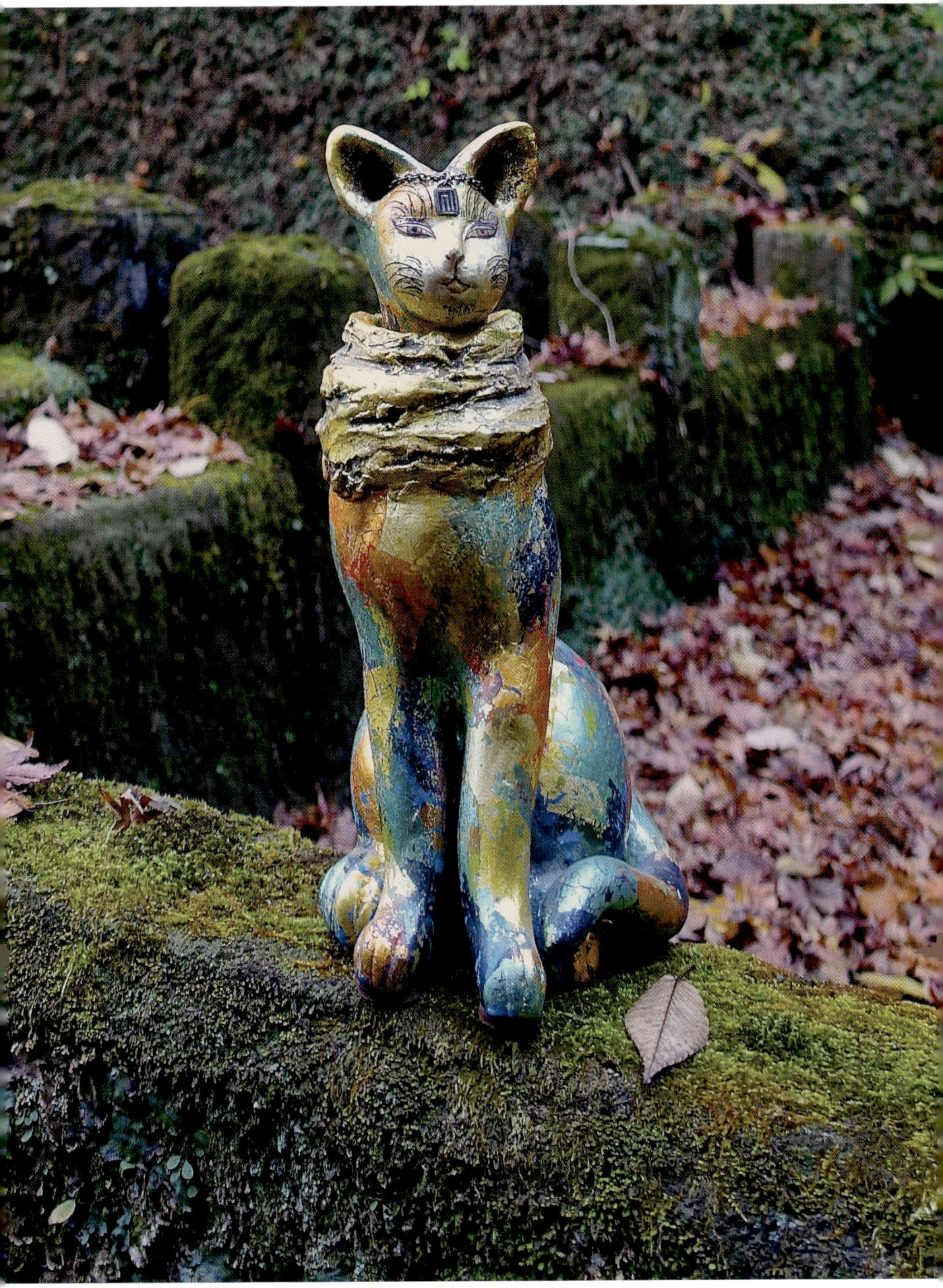

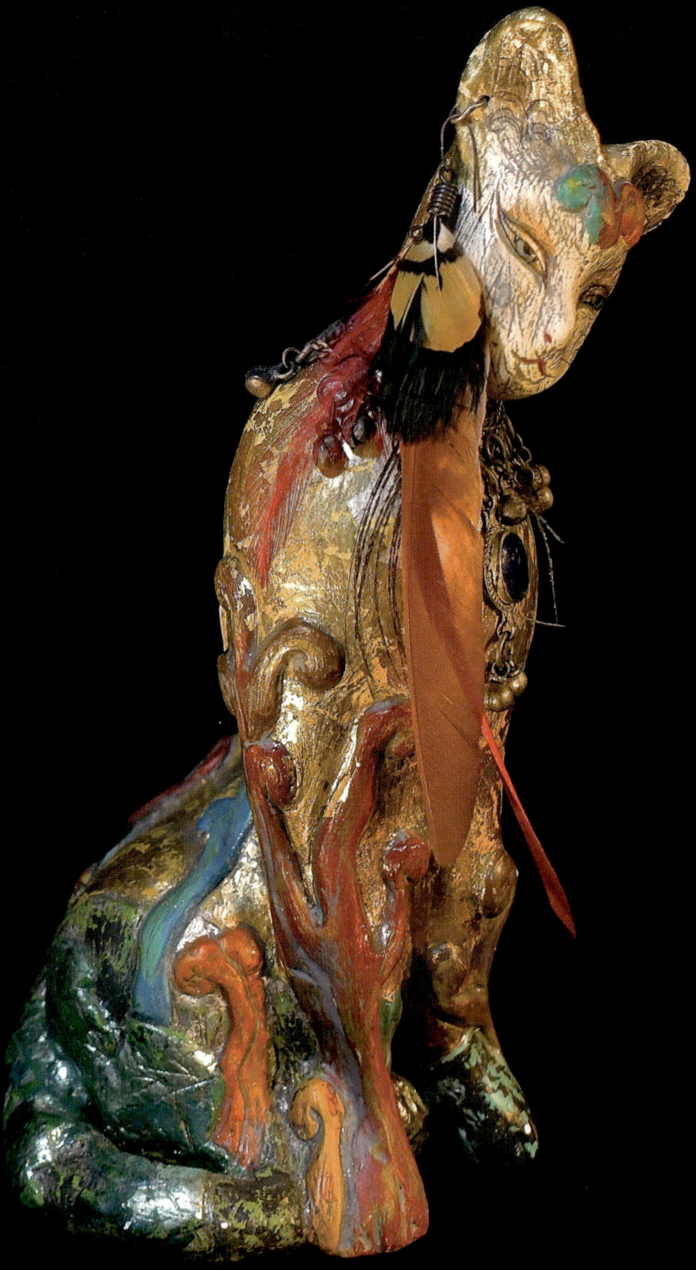

第四十八帖　早蕨（さわらび）

この春は　たれにか見せなむ　亡き人の　形見につめる　峰の早蕨　　中の君
　　（姉君まで亡くなられた今年の春は、お心づくしに下さった父宮ゆかりの早蕨も、
　　今年はお見せする人とてありません）

　姉の大君が亡くなった初めての春、悲しみの中の君に、山の高僧から蕨や土筆が届きます。
　少し痩せた彼女は亡き大君に似てきて、薫の想いは中の君に移ってゆきます。
　薫は、匂宮が中の君を京へ迎える時のお世話もしますが、中の君を匂宮に譲ったことに悔いが出来てきました。

Chapter 48　Sawarabi (Bracken Shoots)

[Nakanokimi] Kono haru wa / Tare nika misenan / Naki hito no / Katami ni tsumeru / Mine no sawarabi
(As even my sister is gone, in this spring I have nobody to show the bracket shoots you brought to me as a kind present reminding of my father.)

In the first spring after the death of her sister Ōikimi, Nakanokimi who is sunk in sorrow receives a gift containing bracket and horsetail shoots from a high priest living in the mountain.
Getting skinnier than before, she now resembles the late Ōikimi. This shifts Kaoru's love gradually to Nakanokimi.
Kaoru assists Niō-no-miya welcoming Nakanokimi in Kyoto, but at the same time regretted that he conceded her to Niō-no-miya.

第四十九帖　宿木 (やどりぎ)

よそへてぞ　見るべかりける　白露の　契りかおきし　朝顔の花　　薫

(白露(大君)が契り残した朝顔(中の君)を、私はやはり亡きお方の形見と見るべきでした)

　帝は娘・二の宮の婿に薫を、夕霧右大臣は匂宮を娘・六の君に婿にと考えました。
　匂宮と六の君の結婚を知り、嘆き悲しむ中の君を慰める薫は、愛した亡き大君を妹の中の君に重ね、恋情を訴えます。
　しかし中の君は懐妊中のため薫はあきらめますが、匂宮は、薫の移り香のする彼女を疑うのでした。

Chapter 49　Yadorigi (Mistletoe)

[Kaoru] Yosohe te zo / Miru bekari keru / Shira-tsuyu no / Chigiri ka oki shi / Asagao no hana
(I should have treated the morning glory (Nakanokimi) promised for me by the morning dew (Ōikimi) as the keepsake from the departed.)

Emperor plans to marry Kaoru to the second princess, while Yūgiri plans to marry Niō-no-miya to his sixth daughter.
Consoling Nakanokimi who is grieving over the marriage of Niō-no-miya and the sixth princess, Kaoru sees the vision of the late Ōikimi he loved overlapped on her sister Nakanokimi, and confesses his love to her.
Kaoru has to give up on her because she was pregnant. However, Niō-no-miya suspects Nakanokimi because of the scent of Kaoru lingered on her.

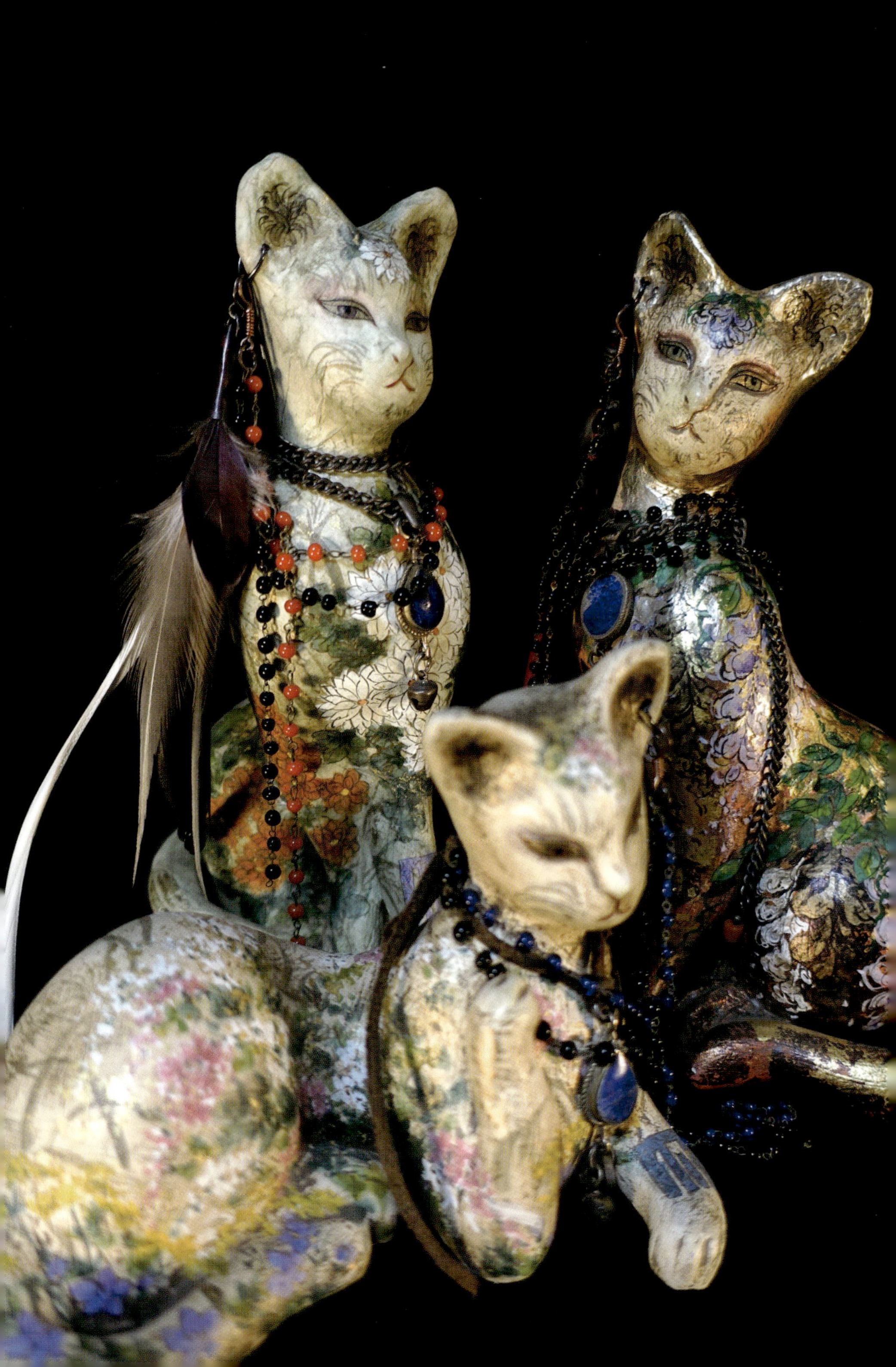

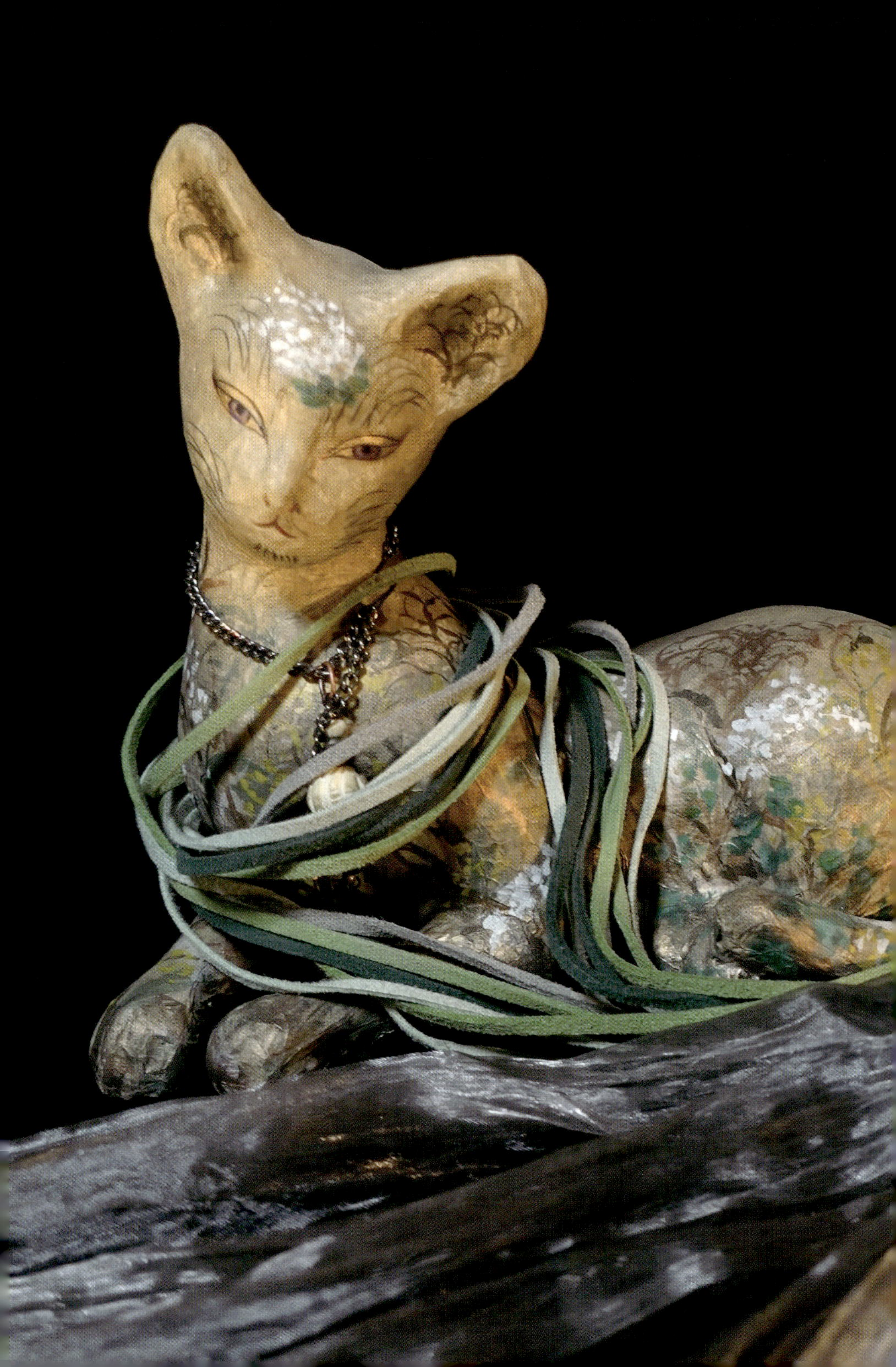

第五十帖　東屋 (あづまや)

形見ぞと　見るにつけては　朝露の　所せきまで　ぬるる袖かな　　　薫

（この人を大君の形見と思いつつ行く道すがら、この袖は川霧と涙でしっとりと濡れることです）

薫は、中の君から大君に似ているという異母妹の浮舟の話を聞いて興味を持ちます。しかし、中の君の邸で浮舟が匂宮の目に留まってしまい、小さな家（東屋）に隠しました。
そこに薫が訪ねてゆき、浮舟を宇治に連れてゆきます。

Chapter 50　Azumaya (Eastern Cottage)

[Kaoru] Katami zo to / Miru ni tsukete wa / Asatsuyu no / Tokoroseki made / Nururu sode kana
(As I walk thinking that she is the memento of Ōikimi, the sleeve of mine is drenched by the mist of the river and my tears.)

Hearing Nakanokimi talking about her half-sister Ukifune who looks quite like Ōikimi, he begins to take interest in her.
However, as Ukifune was noticed by Niō-no-miya in the house of Nakanokimi, people decided to let her hide in a small cottage. Kaoru visits Ukifune in the cottage and takes her to Uji.

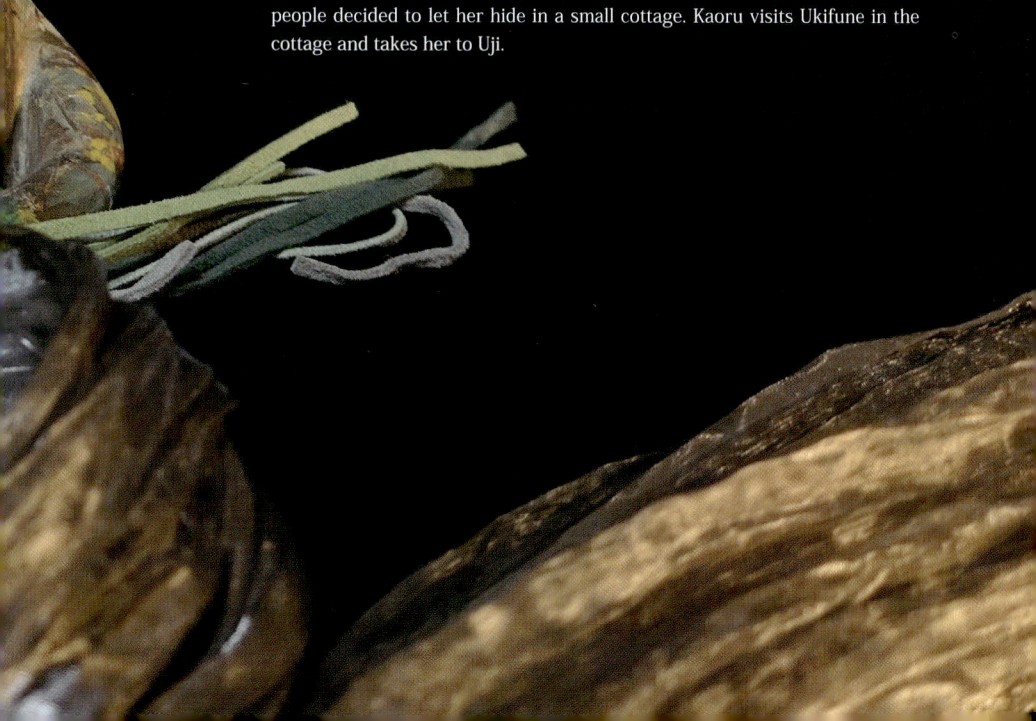

第五十一帖　浮舟(うきふね)

年経とも　かはらむものか　橘の　小島のさきに　契る心は　　　匂宮

　（橘の小島にかけて誓おう、あなたに行く末をお約束する心は変わらないと）

橘の色は　かはらじを　この浮舟ぞ　ゆくへ知られぬ　　　浮舟

　（橘の小島の色は変わらないでしょうけれど、浮舟のようなこの身はどこへ漂って行くのでしょう）

　匂宮は浮舟が薫の恋人となり宇治にいる事を知り、薫の振舞いをして邸に入って浮舟を恋人にしてしまいます。そして浮舟を船で連れ出し、橘の小島で永遠の愛を誓うのでした。
　浮舟は匂宮と薫の間で苦しみ、消えてなくなりたいと思い詰めます。

Chapter 51　**Ukifune** (Drifting Boat)

[Niō-no-miya] Toshi hete mo / Kawaran monoka / Tachibana no / Kojima no saki ni / Chigiru kokoro wa
(I swear upon this islet of orange trees that my mind to promise your future will never change.)

[Ukifune] Tachibana no / Iro wa kawaraji o / Kono Ukifune zo / Yukue shirarenu
(The colour of orange does not change, but I don't know where a flowing boat (ukifune) like me drifts to.)

Niō-no-miya comes to know that Ukifune has become a lover to Kaoru and living in Uji. So he entered the cottage in Uji by disguising himself as Kaoru and made Ukifune his lover. He then takes Ukifune to an islet on a boat and vows eternal love to her.
Torn between Niō-no-miya and Kaoru, Ukifune is so anguished that she wants to be vanished.

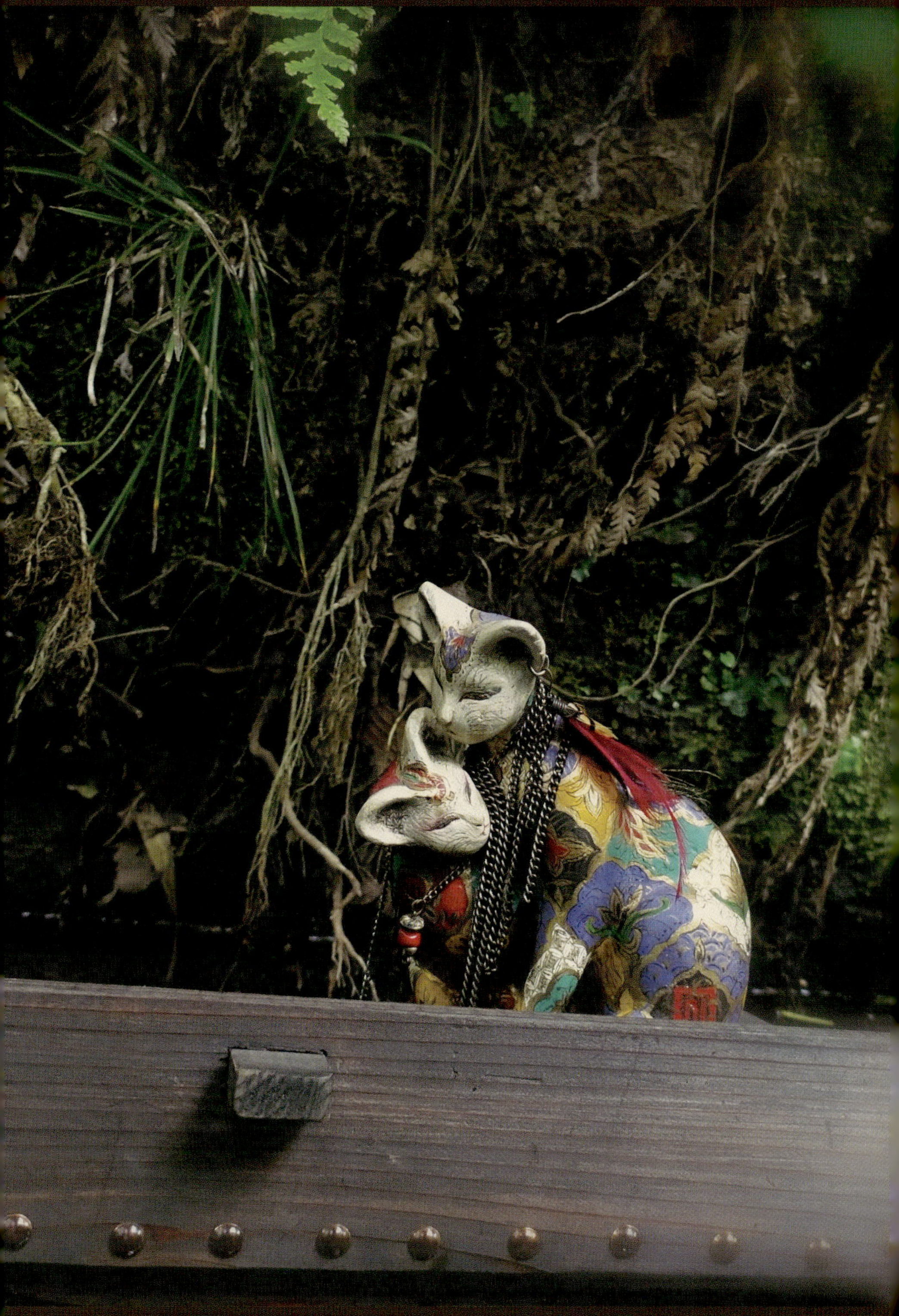

第五十二帖 蜻蛉 (かげろふ)

ありと見て 手にはとられず 見ればまた
行く方もしらず 消えし蜻蛉　薫
(ここにあると見えて手には取られず、わがものとしたと思えば、
また行方も知れず消えて行った蜻蛉よ)

浮舟の入水に薫は嘆き哀しみますが、悲嘆の匂宮を見て、浮舟との仲を確信します。薫は女一の宮の高貴な美しさに惹かれたり、故式部卿宮の姫君の没落した様を見たり、女の運命の哀しさを感じ、また宇治の姫君たちを想うのでした。

Chapter 52　Kagerō (Ephemera)

[Kaoru] Ari to mite / Te niwa torarezu / Mireba mata / Yukue mo shirazu / Kieshi kagerō
(Oh, ephemera, you seemed to be here but cannot be caught by hand. You then reappear but immediately fade out to somewhere I don't know.)

Kaoru mourns for Ukifune hearing the news that she committed suicide by jumping into the water. However, looking at Niō-no-miya also grieving just like him, Kaoru gets convinced that Niō-no-miya had a relation with Ukifune.
Charmed by the noble beauty of Princess Onna-ichino-miya and watching the decline of the daughter of late Prince Shikibukyo-no-Miya Kaoru realises the sorrowful fate of women and reminds of the sisters of Uji.

第五十三帖 手習 (てならひ)

亡きものに 身をも人をも 思ひつつ
棄ててし世をぞ さらに棄てつる　浮舟

(わが身も人もなきものと思って、一度捨てた世を、今また出家してもう一度捨ててしまった)

浮舟は宇治院で横川の僧都に発見され助かり、取られて小野の庵に住みます。浮舟は何も語らず、僧都の妹の尼君に引き取られて手習いなどして日々を過ごします。

そんな中、尼君の親族に求婚され、周囲は喜びましたが、浮舟はわが身の不幸を嘆き、出家することでやっと心の安らぎを得たのです。

Chapter 53 Tenarai (Writing Practice)

[Ukifune] Naki mono ni / Mi o mo hito o mo / Omoitsutsu / Suteshi yo o zo / Sarani sute tsuru
(I once abandoned this world thinking that I and other people are vanished, but I abandoned it again by entering the nunnery)

Ukifune is saved near the Uji-in Temple by priest called Yokawa-no-sōzu. The priest takes her to a nun who is his sister and left her in care of the nun. Ukifune settles in a hermitage called Ono-no-iori and spent the days by doing writing practice, without speaking a word.

One day, a relative of the nun made a proposal of marriage to her, which makes the people around her very glad. However, all Ukifune did is deplore misfortune of herself. She is not unable to feel a peace of mind until she herself becomes a nun.

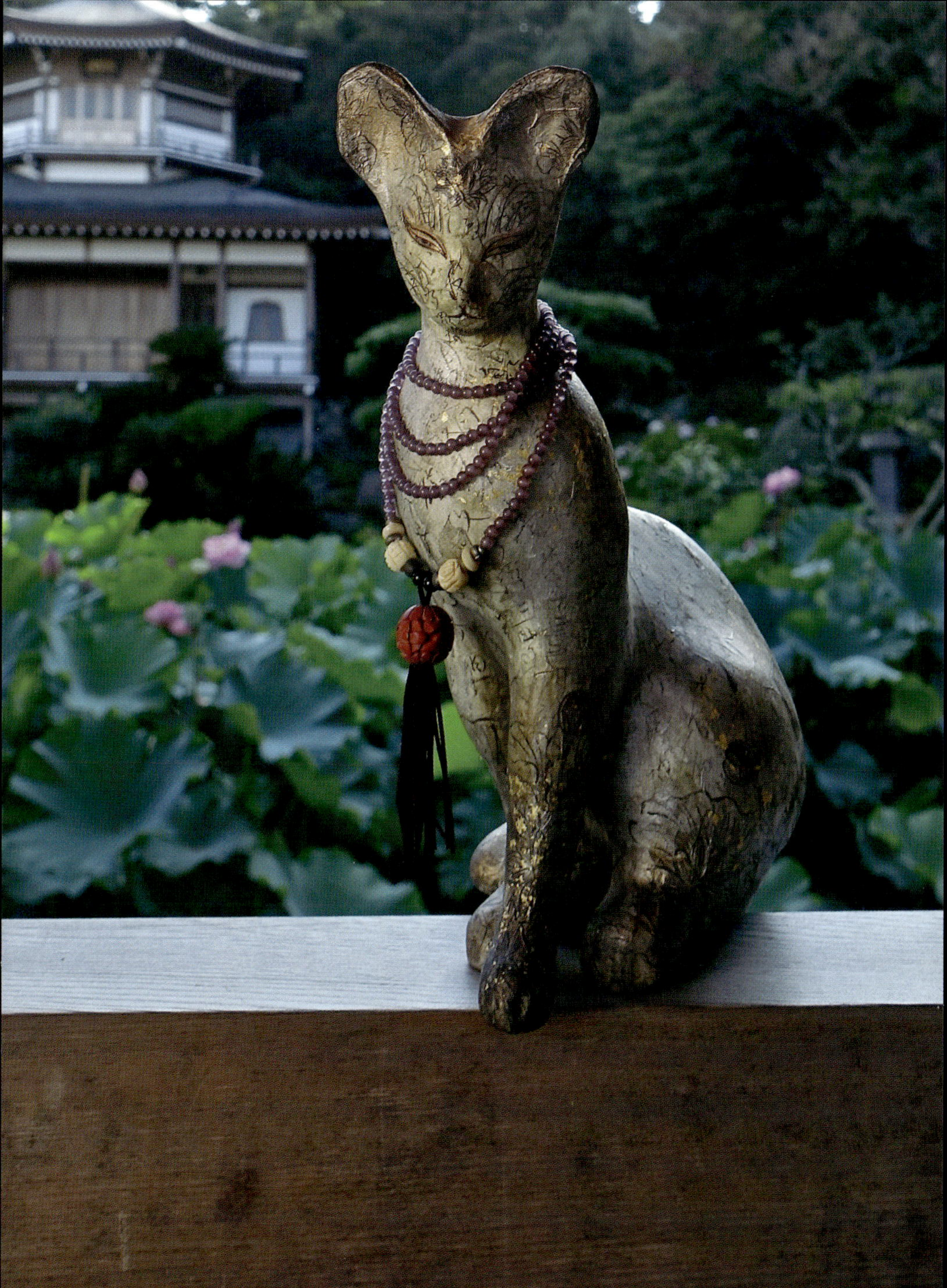

第五十四帖　夢の浮橋(ゆめのうきはし)

世の中は　夢の渡りの　浮橋か　うち渡りつつ　物をこそおもへ　　古歌より

　(世の中は、夢の中で浮橋を渡っているようなものでしょうか。その橋を渡りながら、絶えず思い悩んでおります)

　薫は死んだと思っていた浮舟が、横川の僧都に助けられ、出家して小野にいることを聞きます。浮舟に会いたい薫は、彼女の弟・小君に手紙を持たせました。
　浮舟は薫を想うものの、人違いとして小君との対面も、手紙の返事も頑なまでに拒みます。それは流されてきた浮舟が、最後に自分で選んだ固い意志でした。

Chapter 54 Yume no Ukihashi (Floating Bridge of Dreams)

[Ancient poem] Yononaka wa / Yume no watari no / Ukihashi ka / Uchiwatari tsutsu / Mono o koso omoe
(The life in this world may be like going over a floating bridge in a dream. I am also crossing the bridge with perpetual worries and troubles.)

Kaoru is informed that Ukifune he thought dead was saved by priest Yokawa-no-sōzu and that she is staying in Ono as a nun.
With a wish to meet her, Kaoru asked Kogimi, her brother, to hand her a letter.
Ukifune still loves Kaoru actually but, saying that she is taken for somebody else, she refused to see Kogimi nor receive the letter obstinately.
It is the strong will that Ukifune, who has been drifting for a so long time, selects finally by herself.

●黒揚羽（くろあけは）
光輝くものの闇は深い。
猫の姿を仮た黒揚羽は闇を漂う…

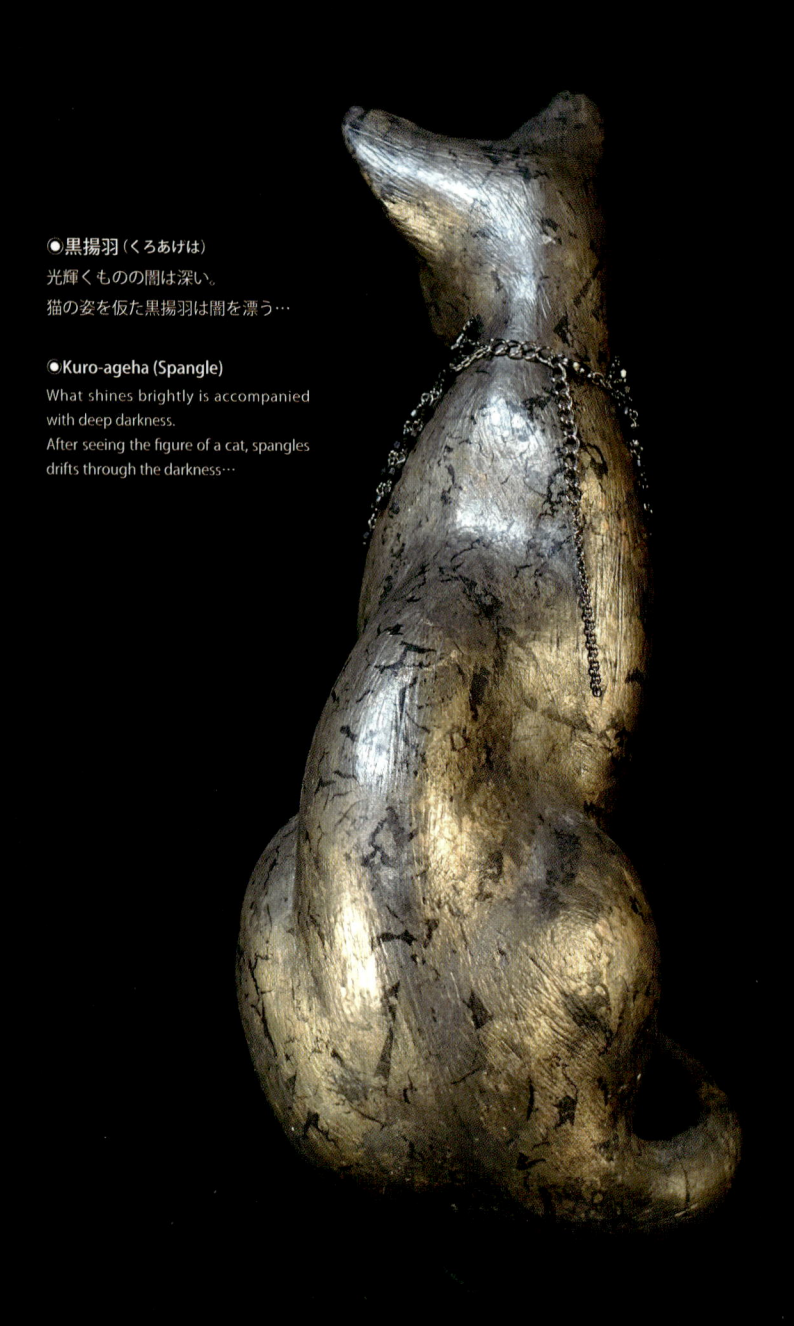

●Kuro-ageha (Spangle)
What shines brightly is accompanied with deep darkness.
After seeing the figure of a cat, spangles drifts through the darkness…

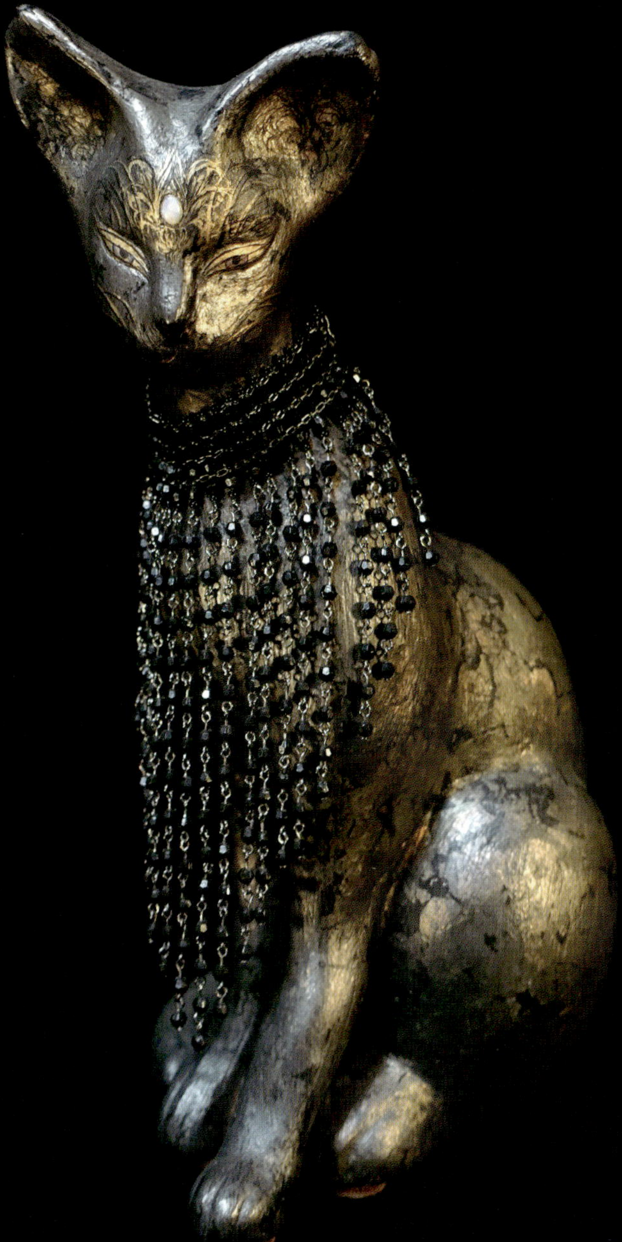

あとがき

或る日、源氏香の鎧をまとったような憂いげな猫が汀に辿り着いただけだった…

蟬丸の「源氏物語」全作品化という壮大なGプロジェクトが歩みはじめた
2004年の10月に第一章が発表され2007年11月の最終章まで
ほぼ4年に渡る創作の旅はとりあえず終わる

現在にいたるまで蟬丸が全作品のオリジナルを保管していることで
より多くの方々にこんな源氏物語の世界があることを
知って頂きたいと制作終了の後も機会あるごとに発表し続けている

今なぜ源氏物語なのか
しかも猫であるのかを考察したが答えは見えてこない
作者本人としてはたまたまそこに猫が居て
紫式部の小説が幸運にも現存していただけ

源氏物語は絢爛たる豪奢な貴族世界の
今と変わらぬヒトの情念と欲望が渦まく超シリアスな物語である故に
猫の姿を仮ることで生々しさを抽象化できるのではないかという単純な動機

あくまでも極私的な解釈による蟬丸源氏物語は一応完結している
が、時は河のように流れている
今回の全作品集の出版を期にスピンアウトの新作も含め
第二次の彷徨いの予感もする

2015　春　蟬丸

Afterword

One day a cat arrived at the shore. It looks like armed in Genji-ko pattern and merancholic. It was a simple event.

But it was the time when the project G started---- a great plan that all episodes of The Tale of Genji into the works of Semimal.
The first chapter released in October 2004, and the last chapter in November 2007. She finished four years journey of creation...for now.

Semimal herself keeps all of these original works at present, so she takes every chanse to exhibit this series, to let people know her world of the Tale of Genji.

Why the Tale of Genji now? Why by cats?
I thought long time but could not find the answer.
As the creator herself, because there are cats and the novel by Murasaki-Shikibu luckely.

The Tale of Genji, sets in the magnificent Imperial Court, is a very serious novel on emotions and desires of human that never change still in our time.
And Semimal thought simply that she can make them abstract. The figure of cat changes their vividness into abstruct form.

The Tale of Genji of Semimal, created by her privatical interpretation, is finished for now.
But time flows like river.
If the publication of this complete works will make her new design like spin-out works of this series.
Semimal's next jouney of creation will begin that time......probably.

Spring 2015 *Semimal*

蟬丸 (せみまる)

1992年 北鎌倉の明月院の谷戸に工房〈蟬丸 Semimal〉を開設
裏山の杉林、谷戸の四季の花華、我が家のネコが蜥蜴、土竜、蝶、
山鳩、兎なんぞを咥えて来た…

1995年	個展中心の作品発表を開始
2000年	倫敦・「大和ファウンデーションgallery」個展
2003年	蟬丸源氏物語 制作開始 〜 2008年〈全27体作品 完成〉
2008年	源氏千年紀 国内各地で個展、企画展を開催
2009年	慈しみのイコン〈BOSATSU菩薩〉シリーズ制作開始
2012年	巴里・「Galerieマレ ウェスト」個展
2013年	東京・目黒「雅叙園」百段階段〈ねこらんまん展〉出品
	巴里と北鎌倉〈パリNEKOコレクション2013〉出品
	〜以降、現在まで
2014年	毎年、恒例の蟬丸工房の《galrie月》- BOSATSU - 個展
2015年	作品写真集『蟬丸源氏物語』上梓

〒247-0062
神奈川県 鎌倉市 山ノ内 207
E-mail semimail@semimal.com
URL www.semimal.com
Face book www.facebook.com/semimalceramicdoll

Semimal

In 1992, Semimal located her atelier "Semimal" in a Yato, a small valley near the Meigetsu-in Temple, Kita-Kamakura.
There is a woods of cedar on the mountain behind the atelier.
Flowers and blossoms of seasons bloom in Yato.
And, her cat hunts and brings her little creatures----lizards, moles, butterflys, dove, and rabbits.

1995	Semimal began to exhibit her works mainly in solo shows.
2000	The solo show at Yamato Foundation Gallery, London
2003	Starts execution of the series of "The Tale of Genji of Semimal" (She finished all 27 works in 2008)
2008	This year is the Millennium of Genji (after a thousand years from The Tale of Genji first appeared in a historical record), and Semimal had solo shows and an exhibition on Genji.
2009	Starts the execution of the series of "BOSATSU: The Icons of Affection"
2012	The solo show at La Galerie Marais Ouest, Paris
2013	Participates in "Neko Ranman" exhibition (Cats are in full bloom) at the Hyakudan-Kaidan pavilion (A Hundred Steps), Meguro Gajoen. Tokyo
	Participates in "Paris NEKO Collections 2013" in Paris and Kita-Kamakura (This exhibition continues 2015)
2014	The seventh solo show of "BOSATSU: The Icons of Affection" at Galerie Tsuki, Kita-Kamakura (The solo show started in 2009)
2015	The publication of the photo book "TheTale of Genji of Semimal"

TH ART SERIES

蟬丸源氏物語

著 者	蟬丸
写 真	higla
発行日	2015 年 7 月 21 日
発行人	鈴木孝
発 行	有限会社アトリエサード
	東京都新宿区高田馬場1-21-24-301 〒169-0075
	TEL.03-5272-5037 FAX.03-5272-5038
	http://www.a-third.com／th@a-third.com
	振替口座／00160-8-728019
発 売	株式会社書苑新社
印 刷	株式会社厚徳社
定 価	本体 2750 円＋税

ISBN978-4-88375-206-5 C0072 ¥2750E

©2015 SEMIMARU, HIGLA　　　　Printed in JAPAN

www.a-third.com